The Story of
British Trade Unions

Katharine Savage   *The Story of British Trade Unions*

Kestrel Books

KESTREL BOOKS
Published by Penguin Books Ltd
Harmondsworth, Middlesex, England

Copyright © 1977 by Katharine Savage

First published 1977

ISBN 0 7226 5410 3
Printed in Great Britain by
Butler & Tanner Ltd, Frome and London

Overleaf: a card issued by the Felt Makers' Union, reputed to be the
oldest trade union in existence – it was established in the seventeenth
century

Contents

1960's -1

1860 - 1900

Acknowledgements

I would like to thank the friends and colleagues who have helped me with this book. Especially I want to express my gratitude to Mark and Jean Abrams who gave me most invaluable advice.

Once more I must record my great gratitude to Gillian Winger. We have now worked together on eight books and I depend increasingly on her with each publication.

The author and publishers would like to thank the following for their kind permission to reproduce illustrative material: Camera Press Ltd for p. 125; Birmingham Public Libraries, Local Studies Department for p. 81 *above right*; Goldsmith Library, University of London, Senate House for p. 72 (photographer Godfrey New); Keystone Press Agency Ltd for pp. 115, 120 *above right*, 133 and 135; Labour Party Library for pp. 66, 86 (photograph by John R. Freeman Ltd), 88, 103 and 118 *left* (Planet News Ltd); Mary Evans Picture Library for pp. 13, 71, and 82 *above right*; National Portrait Gallery, London for pp. 28 *above left*, 40, 51 *above left*, 60 and 78 *below left*; Radio Times Hulton Picture Library for title page and pp. 12, 17, 23, 25, 26, 27, 28 *above right*, 31–32, 37, 43 *both*, 48, 51 *above right*, 55, 74, 78 *below right*, 81 *above left*, 82 *above left*, 83, 93, 99, 100, 102, 105 *both*, 107, 109, 113 *both*, 118 *below left* and 120 *above left*; Royal Commission on the Ancient and Historical Monuments of Scotland for p. 35; The Science Museum, London for p. 18; Syndication International for p. 131; Trades Union Congress Library for pp. 8 and 10 (photograph Leslie Frisby)

The Tolpuddle Martyrs

"WHAT YOU SOWED, WE ARE REAPING"

1 The Tolpuddle Martyrs

Historians have not set a definite date for the formation of the first British Trade Unions. They emerged gradually to establish a new relationship between master and man created by the changing conditions of industry. By the eighteenth century a number of local trade clubs existed in particular towns, and skilled craftsmen met together for mutual support. There was, however, no real organization for negotiating a collective contract between employers and employees on working conditions and wages. From the outset the Trade Unionists aimed to get for their members a fair deal and a reasonable standard of living. Their struggle against traditional government policy and the opposition of the new mill and mine owners was long drawn out, stormy and, at times, violent.

The trial and swift conviction of six farm labourers in the village of Tolpuddle in Dorset in 1834 is the best known example of harsh justice and oppression of workers in early Trade Union history. It showed up the utter helplessness of poor, but honest, citizens to stand up for their rights, and won the sympathy of many fair-minded people.

The tale of the Tolpuddle Martyrs is now famous. At that time there was considerable unrest in many rural areas, particularly in the southern counties. Farm labourers were generally poorly paid, and they bitterly resented the Corn Laws the government had recently introduced, which put a stop to imports of cheap corn from abroad and consequently raised the price of bread.

In desperation, the farm hands carried out hunger riots,

burned the farmers' ricks and broke up farm machinery in order
to draw attention to their grievances. In some districts they
formed village clubs, or Unions, to discuss their problems.
Because these Unions were forbidden by law, they held their
meetings in secret in the back rooms of local inns. The members
took solemn oaths to stand together and conducted their proceedings according to a special ritual which gave an added importance to the occasion.

Landlords around Tolpuddle had recently reduced the wages
of their labourers and they were on the look-out for trouble.
They suspected that the men who joined the clubs were plotting
a rebellion, though they had no real evidence. Suddenly the
landlords took fright and appealed to the local magistrates to
suppress these secret clubs. They acted instantly: the Tolpuddle
police arrested six labourers and threw them into gaol. All six

A watch presented to one of the Martyrs, James Hammett, forty years
after his transportation

were tried for conspiracy and swiftly convicted. It seems that they were simple, peaceable men but they had no means of appealing against the judgement. They could not prove that they were not plotting to disturb the peace and they were sentenced to transportation to Australia for seven years. A few weeks later they found themselves separated from their families and imprisoned in convict ships set for the long, rough voyage to Botany Bay.

The Whig (it would now be called Liberal) government of the day approved of this monstrous action. But many thinking people throughout Britain openly protested at the fate of the Tolpuddle Martyrs; and the cause of Trade Unionism as a means of fighting for a fair deal for wage earners against their employers gained widespread support.

This was an age of dramatic change in Britain, a period in history now known as the Industrial Revolution, despite the fact that it was a slow process rather than a violent event. A whole new field of opportunity was opened up by sensational discoveries of sources of mechanical power. For centuries the British had been an agricultural people, ruled by kings and queens, a Parliament elected by a few thousand people, an established aristocracy and hereditary landlords. Now they were about to be ruled by industrial forces as complex new machines took production out of the hands of men.

The Industrial Revolution dates roughly from the reign of George III, who came to the throne in 1760. The kingdom of Britain was united and stable. The people enjoyed greater freedom than any other European state. Serfdom did not exist; and though a number of the inhabitants were very poor they were freemen and proud of it. They observed the striking differences in living conditions between the proprietors and the peasants, but as there were no hard and fast barriers separating the various levels of society, such as those which existed in France before the Revolution of 1789, the peasants shared to some extent the

11

Cottage spinning, late eighteenth century

way of life of their richer neighbours and there was little class hatred in Britain.

Also, there were no restrictions on the ownership of land. If a labourer saved up money he could buy a plot and farm it just the way he wanted. Those who did not have land of their own and worked for a farmer probably lived with the family, ate at the same table, shared the same pleasures on feast days, and sat in the same pew at church. Naturally there were good masters and bad, industrious labourers and lazy louts. But before the advent of the machine age agriculture was the backbone of life. It united people from every walk of life because they either lived off or worked on the land.

This was the age when cottage industries flourished. Foremost among them spinning and weaving brought in comfortable incomes to country families. Usually the men worked in the fields and the women and children in the home. But sometimes the whole family were spinners and weavers. (The unmarried women were called spinsters, a word that has survived until this day.) They put in long hours, and they often worked in bad conditions. But they were their own masters: they had pride in their work, and they could take a day off to go to the local fair if they wished without asking permission from anyone.

English weavers had learned a lot from Flemish workers, who, fleeing from religious and political strife in their own country, had taken refuge in English villages, bringing with them great experience and skill in their own trade. At first the English weavers cold-shouldered these foreign intruders. But they soon saw that they were hard-working, decent people who settled down, married the local boys and girls and fitted into the English scene.

Most cottage spinners and weavers owned their own wheels and looms, and travelling middlemen supplied them with the raw cotton and wool. The spinners turned the cotton into yarn and the weavers the wool into cloth. Then the middlemen returned and loaded the finished goods on to packhorses who carried them to London, or the ports of Bristol and Hull whence they were shipped to overseas buyers.

An early shoemaker's work-room

Not everyone lived and worked in the country, of course. In the towns, skilled craftsmen were turning out a large variety of artistic and high-quality goods. Goldsmiths and silversmiths, tanners and armourers, shoemakers and tailors, potters and clock-makers, carpenters and builders worked away, sometimes in family units, but usually under a master craftsman who employed several journeymen and trained apprentices. The title 'journeyman' referred to a skilled artisan who had completed seven years' apprenticeship and was fully qualified in his own trade. A journeyman was free to set up his own workshop if he could raise the money. It often happened in novels, and also in real life, that he fell in love with his master's daughter, married her and thus paved the way to independence.

In that age of home-made goods the work of a skilled craftsman was a matter of personal pride and satisfaction. He created each article with his mind and imagination as well as with his hands. Whether it was a pot for the kitchen, a wheel for a wagon, a table or chest, or the most delicate mechanism of a clock, it bore the imprint of individual skill.

In many towns the workers of a single craft formed guilds, or companies, to protect themselves from outside competition, and also, by pooling their knowledge, to improve the quality of their work. They applied to the king to grant them the right to sell goods free of tax within given limits and to tax strangers who came to trade. With royal consent they did good business and built fine halls where they held ceremonial meetings and lavish banquets.

Merchants also formed guilds to increase their trade, for they found that working together they shared the cost of transport and found a larger range of customers for their merchandise. They faded out of existence before the craft guilds, mainly because they were never able to control the vast new markets opened up by the discovery of America at the end of the fifteenth century and the immense riches of India.

By the time of the Tolpuddle trial much of this pre-industrial life had disappeared: the Industrial Revolution had changed the face of Britain. The leisurely way of life had given way to pressurized production. In the old days the happiness of a master craftsman's home and the success of his business depended on the good management of his family, the character of his workmen and the consequent goodwill between master and man.

By the beginning of the nineteenth century many skilled craftsmen had been forced to close down their workshops because they could not compete with the pace of the new machines. At the same time thousands of country people were moving into the towns to work in factories for employers who hired them to do a job and took no interest at all in their welfare.

2 The Industrial Revolution

The Industrial Revolution transformed Britain from a country of peasant occupations and local markets into a largely industrial society feeding trade routes which encircled the globe. This sweeping change in the manner of living came eventually to most European countries. But Britain led the way, mainly because she had a stable government with authority to direct the country, and vast resources of coal which could be used as a new source of energy for the manufacture of iron and cotton goods.

Large deposits of coal had been discovered long before, but it was only during the sixteenth century that mining became a commercial concern. It developed slowly until in the eighteenth century engineers made the important discovery that coal could be used to replace charcoal in the manufacture of iron. Before this discovery British iron foundries had worked in wooded country, chiefly in the southern counties, in order to be close to their fuel supply. But so many trees had been cut down that the forests were barren and by the end of the century the iron industry was in danger of closing down for want of wood.

When the iron manufacturers realized that coal would transform the industry, and that they were no longer dependent on charcoal, they moved their forges and blast furnaces to the midlands and north of England to be near the coalfields. Whole areas became industrialized, factories grew up like mushrooms, the air was black with coal dust and tall chimneys belched out great clouds of smoke. From this 'black country' machines,

The landscape around Wolverhampton in the mid nineteenth century

tools, cutlery, guns, nails, toys, and every kind of house and farm equipment were shipped in barges on a network of newly constructed canals all over England and exported far and wide.

In 1759, the year before George III began his sixty-year reign, James Watt, a young Scottish engineer and inventor, discovered a means of using steam power to drive industrial machines. Men had been working on the theory of using steam power for many years, but their machines always broke down in practice. Watt hit upon the brilliant idea of a separate condenser which cured previous defects. In partnership with Matthew Boulton, a shrewd businessman with a profound faith in the power of steam, Watt perfected his designs. In ten years steam engines were on the market and Britain was well on the way to becoming 'the workshop of the world'.

Meanwhile other men of genius were working on textile machinery. In 1733 John Kay had invented the flying shuttle, and in 1754 James Hargreaves the spinning jenny, both of which

Power-loom weaving in the 1830s

revolutionized the weaving industry. Then in 1769 Richard
Arkwright invented a spinning frame and the British cotton industry led all others. The raw cotton was imported from the
southern plantations of America where it was picked and
packed by African slave labour. The slaving ships had a dis-
graceful but profitable two-way trade, for they carried cargoes
of Negro captives from Africa to the New World and returned
to Britain laden with cotton, sugar and rum.

The need for cottage spinners and weavers with their primitive spinning wheels and hand looms diminished. Home spinning gave way to the mechanization of the cotton industry. The
hand workers could not compete with mass production and
little by little they lost their jobs. Steam uprooted the old cotton
mills which had always been situated on the banks of rivers so
that the wheels could be turned by waterpower. The textile industry moved to factory towns, especially in Lancashire where
the damp climate was well suited to the treatment of cotton,
because it remained pliable and easy to work. The output was

enormous. Sheets and tablecloths formerly reserved for the wealthy became commonplace in many homes. And fine muslin which had previously been imported at great expense from India was manufactured in Britain and sold in shops and markets everywhere.

Men of many trades left the countryside and flocked to the towns. Previously, they had been content to work in outlying villages, selling their skills and their wares to the local inhabitants. Carpenters, masons, shoemakers, blacksmiths and tailors had made a good living. Pedlars had called at farms and put up stalls at the local fairs to supply household needs. But life was changing. Often craftsmen had handed over their goods to be sold by a middleman who took a large share of the profits. Now they listened to tales of wealthy customers in the factory towns and saw the advantage of dealing with them directly.

A mass movement from farms to factories had already begun. It was speeded up by the Enclosure Acts, government measures which gave well-to-do farmers the right to fence in common land for their own use. The government had a purpose in passing these Acts, for it meant that experienced farmers took over poor land and farmed it well. They studied the rotation of crops and reaped good harvests. With a fast-growing population food was urgently needed. During the reign of George III the number of people in Britain rose from $7\frac{1}{2}$ million to over 14 million. Very little food was imported and the country had to live off its own resources.

But these same Enclosure Acts deprived the small farmers of a living. Formerly a man with a few acres had been able to cultivate them for his own household; and at the same time graze his cattle and sheep, and turn out his pigs and geese on the common he shared with the rest of the village. Now he was entirely dependent on his little plot to feed man and beast and there was not enough food to go round.

In addition, because of the changes in the cotton industry,

farmers' wives and children no longer brought in money from spinning and weaving. They were unemployed and very hungry. Therefore country families were forced to sell up their homes, and a sad procession of destitute peasants drifted into the towns seeking work.

In the early days of the Industrial Revolution the transport system in Britain was totally unfitted to cope with the situation. In winter the roads were churned up into almost impassable quagmires or frozen into sheet ice. Wagon wheels sank in up to the axle and packhorses wallowed helplessly in the mud. In summer travellers were stifled by clouds of dust.

Highwaymen knew exactly where trouble was likely to occur, lay in wait for stranded merchants or travellers and robbed them mercilessly. It was obviously impossible to deliver goods on time under these conditions and the people in the towns went hungry if the wagons bringing them provisions from the country could not get through. Towards the middle of the eighteenth century people began to complain and the authorities were forced to take notice. Parliament authorized the building of roads, bridges and canals and more and more people used them. Drivers paid their tolls at the turnpike and coaches ran on scheduled routes. In 1754, what was evidently the most super coach service of the day advertised a four-and-a-half-day journey from Manchester to London. (Today it takes two and a half hours by train, and three quarters of an hour by air.)

The new roads soon put the highwaymen out of business. The forests where they had lurked had been cut down for charcoal or enclosed for farmland. On the coach roads the horses went along at a spanking pace and it was far more difficult to organize a hold-up.

On the face of it the Industrial Revolution was an industrial miracle. It was a process rather than an event; an outward expression of a free people, bulging with genius, enterprise and ambition. It was an intellectual triumph, creative and challenging. By the year 1800 Britain was 'the workshop of the world', dominating world production and trade.

But the human side of this sensational industrial progress was fraught with problems and darkened by suffering. A large proportion of the workers who had made British greatness possible were almost starving. Innumerable families who had lived simply, but contentedly, in humble homes in the country had been caught up in the irresistible wheels of the new mechanical age and crushed.

All over Britain rebellion was brewing and groups of miners and factory workers were beginning to defend their rights. Because they did not own property or have any money in the bank, they had no vote, no voice in running the country and no way of expressing their grievances. But they were becoming conscious of their growing power, for they knew that they manned the machines that made the money for their employers.

The Industrial Revolution had created a rift and a battle between master and man which had scarcely existed before. It was becoming increasingly clear that unless some wise people found a way for employers and employees to meet on equal terms Britain would be ruined by hatred and violence.

3 The Conflict of Classes

For well-to-do families in Britain the eighteenth century was a splendid time. The aristocracy and the gentry owned castles and mansions, parks and farmland. In the second half of the century many of them made fortunes from comparatively poor land which rocketed in value when it was developed as a factory site or a coal mine. During the Napoleonic Wars trade boomed and after 1815 when Prussia and Britain decisively defeated Napoleon's armies at the battle of Waterloo, the country was at peace.

In 1776 the United States of America had cast off British rule and declared their independence, but Britain still reigned over a vast Empire. She counted among her overseas possessions: Australia, Canada, Malaya, New Zealand, parts of India and west Africa, and many other far-flung territories. The Empire builders proclaimed with pride that 'the sun never sets on the Union Jack'. Prosperity seemed indestructible.

But, with a few outstanding exceptions, even the most experienced and far-sighted leaders failed to recognize the pitiful plight of the common man. They did not realize that during the Industrial Revolution two classes were born into British society – a rich middle class and an impoverished industrial working class. Both, in their various ways, were necessary to meet the demands of expanding industry. Factory owners and managers, merchants and shippers, bankers and engineers climbed rapidly from the lower ranks of society to positions of power; whereas many poor, but talented, men and women were

George Cruikshank's view of the state of the British nation in 1840. This picture of cheerful business ignores the desperate poverty of vast numbers of new industrial workers forced into factories where they lost their identity and independence.

Unconsciously the factory workers were moulded into a body of people who, through no fault of their own, sank to the lowest depths of poverty and suffering. In the old days they had been poor, but thrifty, accustomed to accept authority and respectful of their superiors in wealth and learning. But their new bosses were different: money grubbing, impersonal and tyrannical, and they did not respect them at all. For the first time in British history class hatred reared its ugly head.

By 1833 a few people were beginning to analyse the situation. An observer of social and industrial conditions in Britain stated that 'the steam engine had drawn the population together in dense masses', and the poet and social critic William Blake spoke of 'the dark satanic mill'. They saw the problems, but they had, at this time, no solution.

Because the cotton mills were the first factory industries they stand out in history as examples of the average conditions created by the Industrial Revolution. The state of many independent spinners and weavers who had been forced out of work by factory competition was most pitiful. They had no other skill so they could not find alternative work at home. Most of them were reluctant to move because they were used to the country and afraid of life in an unknown town.

Once they arrived in a factory town most of them found a job, but they soon discovered that their living conditions were shameful. Employers were compelled to provide lodging for their factory hands, but they built the dwellings in the cheapest possible way. They were ramshackle and totally inadequate. Whole families lived in one room in the utmost squalor, often without lighting, heating, running water or any form of drainage. Every factory was surrounded by a slum district where the streets were foul with refuse. No one was appointed to inspect the tenement buildings to see if the roofs were leaking,

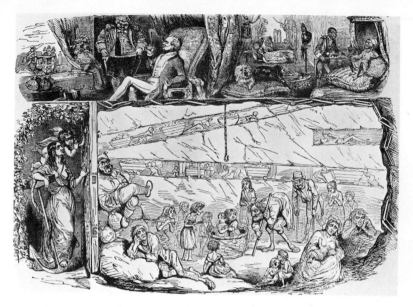

The two sides of industry – Capital and Labour – portrayed in
Punch in 1847

the plaster peeling off the walls, or the rooms infested by rats.

The streets in these areas were so dimly lit that it was unsafe for respectable people to go out at night for fear of cut-throats and robbers. There were very few schools because the children who should have been attending them were working in the factories and mines. Medical care hardly existed in the slums. Most of the doctors lived in the more prosperous parts of the towns, and in the frequent epidemics caused by filth and lack of hygiene a large proportion of people who became ill died unattended.

Factory conditions were similarly bad. Men, women and children were exploited as 'sweated labour', overworked and underpaid. Their staple diet was oatmeal, potatoes, onion soup, skimmed milk, and, perhaps as a treat, treacle and home-brewed ale. Meat was an unheard-of luxury. Children were taken out of orphanages and put to work with no pay at all, and many other children were hired out by desperate parents who were

Explosions from fire-damp were just one of the hazards of mining

so poor that they had to have the money. They worked all hours of the day and night to make money for their employers, and it was not until 1847 that the Ten Hours Act was passed through Parliament limiting the working time of boys and girls under the age of eighteen to ten hours a day.

In general, the conditions in the coal industry were worse than anywhere else, owing to the dirt and fumes in the mines and the constant danger of explosions and falling debris. Until the eighteenth century coal had been less important than wood. Groups of miners had worked out of doors with primitive tools turning over the surface of the land, and scraping up a few tons of coal for winter heating. But once steam engines were able to drive underground pumps to clear the water out of the pits the whole mining situation changed. Landowners formed mining companies and sank shafts deep into the earth. They bored long, tortuous tunnels following the seams of coal. With this new equipment the toll of human life and the sum of human suffering mounted enormously in the mining community. Accidents became so frequent that they were almost taken for granted. It is recorded that a well-known judge familiar with mining problems protested publicly when a coroner did not bother to hold an inquest after an accident. His excuse was that 'it was only the corpse of a collier'.

It was usual for whole families, including women and children, to work in the mines in appalling conditions. Largely owing to the efforts of Lord Shaftesbury, a deeply religious and kind-hearted man, a Tory government passed the first effective Factory Act in 1833, regulating working hours and trying to limit the age of children going down the pits. They soon saw the impossibility of trying to enforce such an Act from Westminster without Factory Inspectors. Most children did not have birth certificates and no one knew how old they were. Therefore Lord Shaftesbury with his colleagues appointed a Commission to examine the Employment of Children and Young Persons. Its report appeared in 1842.

The report disclosed that boys from six years upwards were employed in coal mines to draw trucks laden with coal through tunnels far too low for a grown person to pass. 'A girdle is put around the naked waist, to which a chain from the carriage is hooked and passed between the legs, and the boys crawl on their hands and knees, dragging the carriages after them.'

A harnessed child drawing coal in a mine in 1842.
The passages were sometimes only eighteen inches (45 cms) high

The 7th Earl of Shaftesbury

One of the illustrations to the Shaftesbury Report. It shows girls carrying coal in Scottish mines in 1840

The commissioners also reported that both boys and girls from five to eight years worked in the mines as 'trappers'. They sat in a little hole holding a string in their hands to open and shut the doors that let a draught of air into the mines. A little girl of eight described her day: 'I'm a trapper in Gamber Pit. I have to trap without a light and I'm scared. I go at half past three or four in the morning and come out at five or half past in the afternoon. I never go to sleep. Sometimes if I have a light I sing, but not in the dark. I dare not sing then.'

Conditions varied from pit to pit, but, as there were no rigid regulations regarding working hours, many children were underground for as long as sixteen hours a day, six days a week. As a result of the Shaftesbury Report the government passed a second Act prohibiting women and girls from working in the mines at all, and boys under the age of ten.

As the century wore on the rich became richer and the poor

remained poor. But gradually a radical movement arose in the government to champion the cause of working-class discontent. At the same time certain humane and thoughtful factory owners and social reformers struggled to introduce long overdue reforms.

The workers themselves clamoured for fair wages and better living standards, and a chance to share the practical and pleasant things of life. But they also rebelled against the intolerable arrogance of their employers. They saw that these men had become rich and masterful through the workers' toil. They were kings and captains of sweated labour. According to one outspoken cotton spinner they were 'petty monarchs, absolute and despotic'. They were far removed from the problems of their workers, and there was no longer any possibility of day-to-day friendly meeting ground between master and man.

4   The Reformers

Though the nineteenth century was remarkable for the general neglect of the welfare of the working people, there were a few outstanding members of the clergy and some determined reformers who did everything within their power to bring spiritual comfort and practical aid to the poor and needy. The established Church of England, the Anglican Church, dispensed comfort and charity to many deserving people but failed to reach down into the slums and coal mines. The Anglican ministers were devout and many of them most learned. They administered the sacraments to their regular congregations and followed scrupulously the ritual laid down by the Protestant Church, but they were out of touch with human misery.

There remained in England after the Reformation a Roman Catholic minority, and a most active religious group composed of nonconformists, or dissenters. They were basically Protestants, but in principle they were religious rebels, for they could not accept all the official doctrines. Among them were the Presbyterians who lived mainly in Scotland; the Puritans who emigrated to the United States; the Quakers, the Baptists and, most recently formed, the Methodists. They were all sternly regimented sects, austere both in their religious practice and in their lives, rigidly opposed to any form of self-indulgence or worldly display. They were ardent Christians, but passionate individualists, determined to follow the dictates of their own consciences at any cost. In fact, they suffered for their beliefs, for they were debarred from most official positions and deprived of many ordinary rights by the Church and the state. They were allowed to send their children only to certain schools and were not permitted to preach from Protestant pulpits. Nevertheless they persisted in their independent faiths.

John Wesley, the founder of Methodism, was born in 1703. He was the son of Samuel Wesley, an Anglican minister, and Susannah Wesley, who must have been a very exceptional woman. She had eighteen children, of whom John was the fifteenth, and she gave each one separate religious education every week. By her teaching, example and sheer force of character she

John Wesley

Whitefield preaching in Moorfields, London, in 1742

shaped the pattern of their lives. For a time Wesley worked in Oxford where he founded a Holy Club to bring together men devoted to religion and study the scriptures. The members became known as Methodists because of the strict attention that they paid to the order of their lives, seeking perfection in all things. At first it was a term of derision, but it was later accepted with respect.

In 1735 he went with his brother Charles, also an Anglican minister, to the southern state of Georgia, in America, hoping to work as a missionary with the Indians. However, it proved impossible to get into close touch with them and the mission was not a success. He returned to England dissatisfied and restless.

Wesley had a great friend, George Whitefield, a fine preacher who dedicated himself to helping the working people. When the churches were closed against nonconformists, he preached out of doors, wherever he could gather a congregation. He gave them faith in the love of God and brought them Christian teach-

32

ing in simple words that they could understand. Whitefield soon saw that this was the way to reach the multitudes and appealed to John Wesley to come and help him. Wesley was shocked at the idea of abandoning formal services, but he was rapidly converted to Whitefield's ideas and shared his breadth of vision.

Their work spread all over England and to Scotland and Ireland also. Gradually Wesley gathered a band of lay preachers (i.e. ordinary working men who had not been specially trained as clergymen and preachers) and together they preached to labourers in the fields, dockers on the wharves, miners at the pitheads and factory workers in the slums. They visited the prisons and workhouses bringing consolation to people in the very depths of despair.

Wesley described Methodism as 'a religion of the heart'. It was emotional and moved people to mass enthusiasm. They screamed and fainted at the meetings in an ecstasy of religious fervour. But through these public demonstrations they became Christian comrades, and part of a close-knit community. Men and women who lived in what seemed to be a wholly hostile world suddenly felt that they had a place of refuge within the Church, and it gave them hope and a desire to achieve goodness. They gained confidence and some hope for the future when it had appeared that all the odds were against them. They dressed up their children as best they could and sent them to Sunday School, so young Methodists carried on the message.

Wesley himself travelled constantly. He visited factory towns and impoverished country communities, always on horseback. He crossed the Irish Channel forty-two times and made many trips to Scotland. It is said that as he rode along he read the Bible or other scriptures and left the reins loose on the horse's neck trusting him to choose the right road.

Wesley was a devout Christian, an inspired preacher and a man of the highest personal discipline. He ruled the lay preachers and everyone else who worked for him with a rod of iron, and severely punished any lapse of behaviour. He lived very simply and gave all the money he made from his writings to the poor.

He was also a born organizer. During his lifetime he established Methodism as an enduring faith. When he died in 1791 he had recruited 294 lay preachers, and built up a Methodist membership of 72,000 souls.

Perhaps the greatest strength of Methodism was the wide social span of its appeal. It was far from being only a working-class Church. Though Wesley and his followers set out to uplift their spirits and improve the conditions of the downtrodden masses, they also welcomed members of the new middle class and rejoiced in their conversion. Many leaders of industry, factory owners and managers became ardent Methodists. They attended Methodist meetings and began to meet their workers outside the factory walls, and a gleam of understanding penetrated the darkness of labour relations. The early Trade Unionists and the middle-class Methodists were dissenters against established authority. By the end of the eighteenth century the two groups were faithful though undeclared allies, fighting for the cause of justice and humanity.

When John Wesley died, Robert Owen, the famous reformer and ardent socialist, was just twenty years old. He came of a poor Welsh family and finished his school education at nine. He went to work in a cotton factory and did very well indeed. At nineteen he became manager of a big cotton mill in Manchester. He made a great success of the mill and persuaded his partners to buy other mills in the Scottish town of New Lanark, where there were around 2,000 workers, including 500 children from the orphanages and poorhouses of Edinburgh and Glasgow.

Encouraged by his former success Owen decided to run the New Lanark mills for the welfare of the workers as well as commercial gain for the owners. He gave the factory hands better

The bedroom of a worker's cottage at New Lanark mills

homes and encouraged them to keep them clean and orderly. He started schools for the children and saw that they went to them. He opened a store where people could buy good food at moderate prices and he fought crime and drunkenness. At first the workers were suspicious, but he gained their confidence and respect. Under these conditions they worked well and the Lanark mills prospered. They won an international reputation and men and women interested in social problems came from many countries to inspect his system. The whole scheme broke down when Owen's partners were not satisfied with the 5 per cent profit that they received according to his calculations.

In 1817 Owen began to develop a totally socialistic plan with little practical possibility. He proposed that communities of around 1,200 people should be set up at first in England and gradually all over the world. Families would have separate accommodation, but everything else including education, feeding, amusements and finance would be communal. From the age of three children would be brought up by the community. At first he won some support from the British ruling classes, who had been forced to accept the need for industrial reform. But when, at a large meeting in London, Owen announced his hostility to all the recognized forms of religion people began to regard him with some suspicion.

In order to prove the worth of his ideas on community living he set up a centre in the United States called New Harmony. While he ran it himself it went well, but religious and managerial differences created insuperable obstacles and he had to close it down at a loss of almost all the fortune he had earned.

Despite this failure, when he returned to England in 1829 he found himself in the front rank of labour leaders. His ideas on reform were in tune with the times. Trade Unionism was spreading through every industry, the working class were becoming more outspoken in their demands, and the news of Robert Owen's experiments in active socialism aroused great enthusiasm among the workers.

Though he had not managed to achieve his objective he had opened up great possibilities of putting socialist theories into practice in the factory world. He had shown that men and women worked better if they were well fed, with some free time to enjoy life and the knowledge that they were being honestly rewarded for their labour.

Though most other industrialists regarded Owen as a misguided idealist his work had a lasting effect on British socialism.

In this age of budding reform new figures appeared in Britain and William Cobbett was prominent among them. He was born in 1763 in Surrey, the son of a farmer. He soon left the land and went to work in a solicitor's office. Tiring of the law he joined the army and was sent to Canada. He was promoted to regimental sergeant-major and spent all his spare time studying, for he had had little education. When the regiment returned

William Cobbett

to England he resigned and went to the United States, where he made a modest living by teaching some of the many French immigrants who had come to make a new life in new surroundings.

Cobbett began to write articles on a number of not very serious subjects, and when he returned to England in 1800 he began to edit a magazine called the *Weekly Political Register*. About five years later a new seriousness appeared in his writing as he realized for the first time the anxieties and the profound misery of the working classes. He did not support either of the two established parties – the Whigs or the Tories. Instead he clamoured for reform, and even went to prison for supporting an army mutiny protesting against a reduction in pay. When he emerged he was penniless, but he still held the editorship of the *Register*.

The war against France ended in 1812, and there was widespread unemployment and suffering in Britain. Cobbett produced a cheap edition of the *Register* addressed mainly to the labourers in the midland and northern counties, and suddenly he had become prominent as a mouthpiece for the working classes.

At this time the British government embarked on a campaign of repression and in order to avoid arrest Cobbett fled to the United States. He returned to England in 1819 and during the next ten years produced most of his best-known works. Among them were *Advice to Young Men* and *Rural Rides*, a fascinating account of his travels in southern England. In this book he pointed out the destitution of the farming people and in particular the contrast between the prosperity of the landlords and the poverty of the common people. He was prosecuted by the Whig government, and, refusing to employ legal help, defended himself so skilfully that he won his case.

In 1835, at the age of seventy-one, Cobbett died of influenza and exhaustion. He was a real countryman, deeply devoted to the land and intensely patriotic. It was this patriotism that compelled him to defend the rights of the country people, who were downtrodden by the oppression of war and the changes brought about by the Industrial Revolution.

5 The Revolutionaries

There were in Britain during the Industrial Revolution two groups of people concerned in establishing the rights of the working class and in raising the standard of living. They had the same object in view, but they approached it very differently.

One group was made up of social reformers – sober, law-abiding citizens who foresaw a gradual process of advancement, step by step on the rugged road from poverty to prosperity.

The second group was led by social revolutionaries who believed that the only possible way to change the existing conditions was by outright revolution.

The French Revolution which erupted in 1789 raised both hopes and fears in Britain. The despotic rule of the French kings and the gross extravagance of the French court had stirred up considerable criticism in neighbouring countries, and the feudal treatment of the French peasants had aroused indignation in Britain. When a ragged mob stormed through Paris and seized the Bastille many level-headed British leaders thought that a change of French government might not be a bad thing. But when France was racked by violence and bloodshed most of them turned against the Revolution in alarm.

Certain men of unshakeable convictions stood out from the rest and made their mark on public opinion. Foremost among them at this crisis in European affairs was Tom Paine, an English writer and student of both politics and people. He wholeheartedly supported the principles of liberty, equality and fraternity, the war cry of the revolutionaries.

Thomas Paine

Tom's father had been a small-scale farmer, and as a young boy Tom had worked in the fields. When he was fourteen he ran away from home and made his way to London where he got a job in Kew Gardens. As he grew up he led a varied and adventurous life, ending up as a political journalist. At first he was conservative in his outlook, but once he became aware of working-class hardship he turned radical.

Paine was a fine writer and fearless, prepared to suffer for what he thought was right. He paid large fines and went to gaol for expressing his opinions. Through his writings he became an outstanding leader of working-class thought and rebellion, opposed to hereditary rights for kings, nobles or any other privileged persons because they had not earned them. During the

40

War of Independence he spent some years in America and took part in the framing of the United States Constitution. He returned to Europe and in 1792 published his personal beliefs in a book entitled *The Rights of Man.*

Paine readily accepted the abolition of the French monarchy, for he felt most strongly that every citizen of every country should have the right to vote for the government of his choice. He was a passionate advocate of freedom of thought, speech and action. Moreover he believed that every single individual should have an equal chance to live with dignity and prove himself worthy of respect.

The Rights of Man had a wide circulation, particularly among labour leaders who were seeking change and betterment. It came out at a time when working people were beginning openly to question the whole purpose of their lives, and there is no doubt that Tom Paine helped to set the labour movement in action.

Almost three decades after the appearance of Paine's enormously influential book, the most important figure in the history of world socialism was born in Prussia of Jewish parents. Karl Marx's father was a lawyer, greatly interested in social philosophy and religion. Before Karl's birth in 1818 he and his wife had renounced Judaism, adopted Christianity and been baptized as Protestants.

Their home lay near the French frontier and during the Revolution many homeless refugees crossed into Prussia and settled there. So it happened that, as a boy, Karl listened to long and heated discussions on the rights and wrongs of revolution. He studied history and philosophy at university and chose journalism as a career. He soon became editor of a Cologne newspaper with a liberal policy.

In July 1843 Karl Marx married Jenny von Westphalen, the daughter of a senior government official. They loved each other deeply and she was utterly devoted to him during long years of exile and continual hardship. Soon after the marriage his journal was suppressed because he criticized social conditions in Prussia and the Protestant Church. Marx and his wife moved to Paris where they joined a circle of ardent socialists.

In 1848 rebellion was brewing in Prussia against the dictatorial rule of King Friedrich Wilhelm. Socialist theories were becoming popular and Karl Marx was able to go home. At this time he published *The Communist Manifesto*, a summary of his whole social philosophy.

But Friedrich Wilhelm succeeded in crushing his opponents and soon exiled Marx as a dangerous political agitator.

The first English edition of *The Communist Manifesto* appeared in 1850, a time of considerable unrest. It was the fruit of years of study and a carefully considered analysis of the social injustice of Marx's day, working up to the drastic remedy of total revolution.

The Communist Manifesto contained five fundamental ideas. Briefly stated they are:

1. From the beginning of human society all history is the history of class struggle. This struggle can only be ended by communism; when the victory of the working class, or proletariat, over the middle class, or bourgeoisie, will set society free once and for all. In a classless world no man will be in a position to exploit another and there will be no cause for conflict.

2. Human beings have progressed through the years from one stage of civilization to another. Feudalism gave way to capitalism; but capitalism created modern industry which led to the exploitation of the working class. Capitalism will be succeeded by communism.

3. The working class will, and *must*, become the ruling class.

4. The victory of the working class will inevitably lead to a classless society where the state will wither away.

5. There can be no half measures. Communism is the only system of government with a party programme based on the

complete overthrow of capitalism. Socialism, in its various forms, is a stage on the road to communism. But it can never be an end in itself for, to the true Marxist, socialism is pointless because it is concerned with gradual reform of existing conditions instead of total revolution.

Marx did not disguise his threat to the existing order of life and he ended the *Manifesto* with an outright declaration of class warfare: 'Let the ruling classes tremble at the communist revolution. The proletarians have nothing to lose but their chains. They have a world to win. Workers of the world unite.'

Later he published his most famous book, *Das Kapital*. It contained his detailed views on the capitalist system and the prophecy that because it was so evil it was doomed to self-destruction.

After his exile from Prussia Marx arrived in London with no money and no job; and his views were too extreme to have much popular appeal. He wrote a few articles for an American newspaper, but if it had not been for the generosity of Friedrich

Friedrich Engels   Karl Marx

Engels, a fellow philosopher and friend whom he had met in Paris, the family would have starved, for no matter how much they suffered he would not abandon his self-appointed task of righting the wrongs of the age he lived in. As it was, three of his children died in England, among them Edgar, his only son.

Engels was the son of a German textile manufacturer who had come to England to manage the Manchester branch of the family firm at a period when the cotton business was most profitable. At the age of forty-nine he retired in order to devote himself to political writing. He shared many of Marx's ideas and ideals and had helped to draft *The Communist Manifesto*, but he enjoyed life and the things that money could buy and he was not in a hurry to change the whole system. It was a curious contradiction that he willingly received a good salary from the textile industry, a part of the social set-up that he utterly condemned. Moreover, the money he gave to the Marx family came from the same source, so the proceeds of the hated capitalist system paid their meagre bills.

During the nineteenth century socialism spread in Britain, but in a far more moderate form than Karl Marx would have wished. It did not lead, as he had visualized, to a total take-over by the working class and the collapse of capitalism. The early Trade Unions and the parliamentary representatives of working people worked out a strategy for using their growing power without violence. Communism later became a power to be reckoned with, but it has not revolutionized British society; nor has it united the workers of the world. Marx was mistaken in his view that communism would take industrial nations by storm. In fact the first people who fulfilled his dream of total revolution were the vast, illiterate peasant population of Russia, then the most backward nation in Europe.

Jenny Marx died in 1882 and her husband fifteen months later. He had been ill for a long time, but he drove himself mercilessly and by the end he was utterly worn out.

6   The Crime of Conspiracy

Centuries-old English laws had forbidden wage earners to get together, or combine, to discuss their pay and their conditions of work. The Acts which prohibited these meetings were known as the Combination Acts. The workers were expected to accept whatever their masters thought fit and be thankful. But England was supposed to be a free country and the workers saw no good reason to hide their grievances. Journeymen who were skilled artisans in their trades persisted in forming combinations, though it was against the law, to sort out their problems and calculate their just demands. They well knew that they ran the risk of arrest and imprisonment for the crime of conspiracy, but they refused to submit to laws which they considered unfair.

Sidney and Beatrice Webb, prominent reformers and writers, relate in their history of Trade Unionism how, during the eighteenth century, these combinations of workers met under cover of darkness in a corner of a neighbour's field, in a disused quarry or in some lonely wood. The proceedings were held in the greatest secrecy, the records were locked into boxes and buried in remote places, and they took oaths of eternal loyalty and made mystic signs of brotherhood.

The Combination Acts had been passed because in those days it was assumed that it was the business of Parliament and the law courts to regulate the conditions of industry. The government decided the terms of service, the rights of journeymen and the arrangements for apprenticeship. Therefore it followed that any private agreements which conflicted with a parliamentary

45

decision would be considered illegal. In actual fact the police were neither very numerous nor very vigilant and a number of combinations were tolerated, provided they did not cause any trouble.

However, in 1799 the situation changed dramatically for the worse. A Tory government, headed by William Pitt who had become Prime Minister at the early age of twenty-four, brought in Combination Acts which were very much more severe than those that had existed formerly. Supervision was considerably stricter and the penalties far heavier. This came at a time when the full force of the Industrial Revolution was hitting the country as a whole and the workers found themselves confronted by a stone wall of suppression.

Even then the employers were not satisfied and the following year the restrictions were tightened with the object of making it virtually impossible for workers to make a combined appeal for higher wages, or to protest if their wages were reduced. The injustice was evident, for an employer could lay off a part or the whole of his working force if they would not accept the wages he chose to offer. But, on the other hand, the workers could be prosecuted at the slightest sign of resistance to a reduction of wages or worsening of factory conditions.

It is true that the law also forbade combinations of employers, but in practice they had no need to combine because they were already in such a strong position.

In the wake of the French Revolution many leading English-men regarded any sign of a workers' Union with terror, lest it develop into a mass rebellion. Therefore they considered the Combination Acts an absolute necessity for the preservation of law and order. It was openly stated by a judge in a court of law that all such societies were only cloaks for the people of England to conspire against the state, and no one dared dispute what he said. The records show that journeymen were rarely prosecuted unless their employer charged them with conspiracy; but once he decided to do so they were absolutely defenceless.

Early in the nineteenth century a number of cabinet-makers, hatters, iron-founders, cutlers, ribbon-makers and workers in many other trades were arrested and accused of an intention to strike. This was simply a screen because they were actually charged for belonging to a combination. The journeymen printers working for *The Times* newspaper received severe sentences for the same offence. They claimed that they were members of a friendly society which met from time to time for a social evening at the local inn, but their evidence was disregarded. Shoe-makers, calico printers and coach-makers suffered the same fate. In 1816 seven scissor grinders were sentenced to three months' imprisonment because they belonged to a 'Misfortune Club' which helped members of the trade if they were sick or out of work.

The spinners and weavers suffered terribly. From time to time they were so desperate that they broke up machinery or went on strike. But their uprisings were always crushed and they were forced to accept whatever terms their employers dictated. Francis Place, a master tailor who became very prominent in Trade Union action, wrote: 'The sufferings of persons employed in the cotton manufacture were beyond credibility. They were drawn into combinations and then betrayed, prosecuted, convicted, sentenced and were reduced to and kept in the most wretched state of existence.' The industry was so large that most of the factory owners, instead of being promoted workers who had some idea of working conditions, were investors who were in the business solely to make big profits on their capital. They expected their managers to buy labour at the cheapest possible price and so their gain would be greater.

The coal miners were perhaps worse off than all the other workers. Though they made an essential contribution to the progress of the Industrial Revolution they were regarded as un-

A contemporary lampoon on the Luddite leader, shown disguised as a woman. This was no doubt meant by the cartoonist to bring ridicule to 'King Ludd'

skilled labour and kept in a state of complete subjection. They were forced to sign on for at least a year and if they tried to leave for any reason whatsoever the courts treated it as a criminal offence, punishable by a long term of imprisonment.

In 1811 working-class indignation came to a head and organized bands of rioters raided factories and wrecked the machinery. These gangs were known as Luddites because they obeyed the orders of 'King Ludd', a real or imaginary leader. His exploits were heard with bated breath, but he was never identified. The riots began at the lace-making town of Nottingham as a protest against the changeover from hand work to machines.

The Luddites were masked and they operated at night, attacking machines, but not people. The violence spread to other industrial towns until in 1813 the authorities held a mass trial at

York when many Luddites were hanged and others transported to convict camps overseas. It may be that the real King Ludd was among them, for the organization fell apart. 1815 was a bad year in England: the Napoleonic War ended and the price of manufactured goods fell, bringing down the level of wages. Added to this, the farmers had the worst recorded harvest in their history and the price of bread soared. The discontent was so serious that in some districts employers in different industries, in open defiance of the Combination Acts, banded together and agreed on a general wage reduction. The workers were forced to accept this combined ultimatum, for they had no possible alternative. Rioting erupted once more at Nottingham, and fanned out over almost the entire country. Finally even the employers began to acknowledge that wages had sunk to a deplorable level.

At this time of unrest and deep despair the opposition to the Combination Acts gained in Francis Place a most able, courageous and resolute champion to fight its battles and bring fresh hope to thousands of working homes.

7 Francis Place in Action

Francis Place, the man who did more than any other person to abolish the Combination Acts and promote the early Trade Union movement in Britain, was a Londoner all his life. He was born in 1771 in a debtors' prison managed by his father who was bailiff to a local court. Francis grew up the hard way. His father was tough and unstable. He knocked his sons about and gambled away his earnings. From time to time he left home for months on end and his wife supported the family by taking in sewing.

But Francis had one great advantage in life. He was sent to school from the age of four to fourteen, an unusual privilege in those days for a son of a poor family. He always loved learning, he studied well and became head boy of the school. Out of school hours he spent his time in the streets with the other boys of his age. He played street games and took part in gang warfare. He was sturdy and strong and held his own at a time when there was no well-organized police force and crime was rampant. He seems to have developed a sense of right and wrong at an early age, and never got into trouble.

When Francis left school he was apprenticed to a breeches-maker, at a time when leather breeches were very popular because they were so hard wearing – in poor homes they became a family possession to be handed down from father to son. At the age of eighteen he became a qualified journeyman in his own trade. A year later he married Elizabeth Chadd, a girl of sixteen, who was lovely, but also poor. They moved into one room in the Strand where they struggled for a bare living.

Francis Place   Thomas Hardy

Francis Place worked for a master tailor. He collected the
leather from his shop, made the breeches at home and returned
them on time. He was paid for piece-work, but he never had
the security of a regular living wage. Somehow he was persuaded
to join a Breeches Makers' Society, and he regularly contributed
a small sum to help the members when they were ill or bury
them if they died. He did not attend the meetings and he had
no idea that his fellow breeches-makers were about to strike
for better pay. But because he was a member of the Society
he was sacked with the rest when they went on strike.

In the months that followed Elizabeth and Francis Place
suffered almost overwhelming hardship and unhappiness. They
were destitute and their first child died of smallpox. Neither of
them ever forgot the hopelessness of this period of their lives.
Though they were reduced to near starvation they never lost
their personal pride, nor he his resolution to make good. They
went out very seldom, but when they did, they put on the only
decent clothes they possessed and their neighbours regarded
them with envy.

The strike failed because the Society did not have sufficient funds to keep its members alive. The employers took them back on the old terms, with no wage increase. However, Francis Place returned to breeches-making with a will. He worked sixteen to eighteen hours a day, and his wife with him. They were determined to earn enough money for a home where they could bring up children in cleanliness and comfort.

After serious consideration he joined a recently formed combination, the London Corresponding Society. He made the decision with full knowledge of the risks involved, but by now he was deeply conscious of working-class weakness and this kind of Society appeared to be the only way to attract the notice of Parliament and 'public-spirited individuals'.

Though the members of the Corresponding Society were mainly serious-minded, peaceable men the organization was highly suspect. The Tory government, headed by William Pitt, responsible for the Combination Acts of 1799, had been in power for many years. It was made up of aristocratic and well-to-do citizens, deeply entrenched in tradition and privilege and stubbornly opposed to any change.

In the tense years after the French Revolution and during the war with France it was easy to accuse anyone in Britain who questioned the wisdom of the existing regime of being an enemy of the state. The government considered the members of the Corresponding Society as troublemakers and threw many of them into prison. Thomas Hardy, a shoe-maker, and founder of the Society, was tried for high treason and it was feared that he would be sentenced to death. Feeling ran high throughout the country, and though most people were anti-revolutionary they believed in his innocence. The trial went on for nine days of mounting tension. There was great rejoicing in London when Hardy was finally acquitted. Gradually the danger defeated the cause and the Society fell apart. But during his membership Francis Place had observed the process of the law and learned some useful lessons.

52

He had always been a great reader. Even in the darkest days he had managed to borrow books though he could read them only by daylight as he did not have money to buy candles. Now that he was earning a living wage he began to buy them and to collect the library that he treasured for the rest of his life. He read philosophy, history and politics. He learned French in order to study the French reformers Voltaire and Rousseau. He meditated on the role of governments and on the social sciences, and he chafed against the lack of representation for the working people. He was utterly opposed to violence and in favour of legality; but he was prepared to manipulate the existing laws, and use them for what he considered was the public good. He saw that it was hopeless openly to oppose a strong government, and he began to look for other ways and means of bypassing the Tory establishment.

A few years after the end of the strike Place decided that the time had come to stop working for an employer who took all the profits, and to set up on his own as a master tailor. He knew that he was capable of running a business, and he was determined to make up to his wife for all her hardship and give his children a good education. He found a partner who was as poor as himself, and together they opened a shop in Charing Cross Road, an up-and-coming district in the centre of London. Things went fairly well until his partner cheated him and took over the business.

Elizabeth Place was devastated, but her husband was undeterred. He collected a few customers, borrowed some money and bought a larger shop in the same street. At first it was hard going. The family lived from hand to mouth and some of the customers did not pay their bills. But Place's talent for organization stood them in good stead. He gave up, for the present, all thought of taking part in public life and devoted all his brains and energy to making money by honest means. Through sheer hard work and good management he scored a great success. In a few years he had paid off all his debts and was earning a handsome income.

In 1817, at the age of forty-six, Place retired and handed over the shop to his eldest son. By this time he had had fifteen children, ten of whom were still living. In those days of limited medical knowledge and skill, combined with the general lack of hygiene, a great many children did not live to grow up. A medical report from Sheffield in 1839 showed that more than half the babies born to poor parents died before they were five years old.

It was a bad time for business and every other kind of work in Britain. The end of the Napoleonic War had cut down the need for a number of manufactured goods, including uniforms. Four fifths of the tailors were out of work. The country districts were hard hit by the almost total failure of the 1816 harvest, and pathetic groups of labourers travelled from one village to another seeking jobs. Some tried to make their way to the Welsh coalfields hoping to get work in the mines, but many were so weak from hunger that they did not reach their destination.

Francis Place did not need to listen to the working-class tales of distress. He knew them by heart from bitter, first-hand experience and he deeply resented the attitude of the Tory government which took little action to relieve the situation. This post-war period encouraged radical agitators, William Cobbett foremost among them, to whip up working-class solidarity by mass meetings and organized marches. But Francis Place took no part in them. Though he had concentrated on business since he set up on his own, he was known to be a wise and sympathetic friend of the working people. The room behind the shop, lined with the books he loved so much, became a meeting place for politicians and reformers from many walks of life. There they knew they could speak freely and listen in safety.

In 1819 the British people were shocked by the massacre of Peterloo. No one quite knows whether the government intended to stamp out public meetings by an example of force or whether

The Peterloo massacre as portrayed in a contemporary cartoon

the local authorities panicked at the last moment. On 19 August in St Peter's Fields in Manchester 60,000 people gathered to demand the reform of Parliament and a vote for the working man. The meeting was addressed by Henry Hunt, known as Orator Hunt because of his eloquence, and one of the few extremists to become a Member of Parliament for a short spell.

There were a great many women and children in the audience, no one was armed and there was no sign of a disturbance. It may be that the Manchester magistrates feared violence, for they ordered in the Yeomanry, a civil guard composed of businessmen and shopkeepers, to seize the speakers. The Yeomanry showed no mercy: they attacked the audience as well as the speakers and cut them down with their swords. The magistrates then ordered in the Hussars, mounted soldiers of the regular army, to charge the crowds. In ten minutes St Peter's Fields were deserted except for the dead and wounded. Twelve people died and hundreds were injured. The battle got the name of Peterloo for its tragic contrast to the battle of Waterloo fought four years before. There is no doubt that public indignation at the massacre strengthened the cause of reform.

Soon after Place retired from business the general state of the country and the evident and urgent need for the repeal of the Combination Acts drew him back into the political field. He protested openly to employers in his own trade and others at the conditions of their workers, and he wrote articles for any paper that was willing to print his views. He had won a reputation as an able organizer, a well-balanced critic and a modest leader, trusted by men of many trades. He had an exceptional character, for though he wanted to get things done he had no desire or ambition to become a prominent public figure. He knew the value of remaining in the background, pulling important strings behind the scenes and allowing others to take the credit for the changes he brought about.

In the early 1820s Place gained an important ally in his campaign to repeal the Combination Acts. The man was Joseph Hume, a Member of Parliament, and leader of the small group of really liberal members of the Whig government. Place and Hume saw eye to eye on many matters and they decided to play a waiting game.

In 1822 Place considered that the time had come to test their power. Accordingly Hume announced his intention of presenting a Bill to the House of Commons to make it legal for workers to emigrate if they wished to find work abroad; to permit trade societies to negotiate terms of service; and lastly, though he purposely did not lay great stress on this point, to repeal the Combination Acts. The announcement did not arouse great excitement, and Hume succeeded in getting permission to form a Select Parliamentary Committee to discuss the Bill. Between them Hume and Place managed to pack the Committee with men who shared their ideas and who could be trusted to vote the way they wanted. Most of the other Members of Parliament were not interested anyway.

As Place was not a Member of Parliament he did not sit on the Committee, but he followed the proceedings most studiously and not a single sentence escaped his notice. Witnesses were summoned from all over the country, and workers of many trades gave evidence of injustice and the vital need for reform. They were suspicious of all employers, but Francis Place had won their confidence. He saw them all before they appeared before the Committee, heard their cases and briefed them. He calmed down their passionate resentment and put their just demands into words that would not arouse violent opposition in government ranks. For the three months the Committee was sitting he worked night and day.

When the Committee made the final resolution the members voted exactly as Place and Hume had hoped, in favour of the Bill. The evidence had been so sound and reasonable that Hume was able to pass it on to Parliament by general consent. The whole affair had been carried out so quietly within the law, without publicity or fuss, that it slipped through the House of Commons and the House of Lords without a debate or a division. Later when the government realized that the Combination Acts were no longer in force many members angrily accused Hume of 'smuggling' in the Bill. But it was then too late for official action.

In 1825 the Bill became law and together Francis Place and Joseph Hume had made a masterly move towards social justice.

8   One Man One Vote

Francis Place had been absolutely right in his determination to abolish the Combination Acts, for they were cruel, unjust and ineffective. He was, however, mistaken in his forecast of the immediate effect of this newly won freedom on the working class.

His intensive study of the conditions and behaviour of people and governments had convinced him that the underground combinations had arisen in defiance of intolerable oppression as a hazardous bid for liberty against evil management and ruthless money power. Because of this belief he predicted that once the workers were free to meet openly to discuss their problems, without fear of fines or imprisonment, they would not find it worthwhile to form trade societies as they would serve no useful purpose. His optimistic vision of working men's delegations approaching their managers to settle terms of employment with goodwill on both sides turned out to be a vain hope.

Once the workers heard of the repeal of the Combination Acts they released their pent-up anger and long-standing resentment in widespread demonstrations and strikes. They reckoned that if it was right to put an end to the Acts in 1825, it would have been equally just to repeal them fifty years earlier. They decided that their employers owed them a massive debt and that this was the moment to collect it.

In one industry after another workers rebelled as they had never dared before. The cotton spinners and weavers at Glasgow and Manchester left their wheels and their looms and threatened never to return unless their claims were accepted. The cutlers at Sheffield were fully employed, but they were overworked and underpaid. They demanded double the money they had been earning for a three-day working week. And the young seamen apprentices of Sunderland, a big shipping area, went ashore and refused to reboard their ships until they were guaranteed tea and sugar with their other rations.

The factories were chaotic. The employers still held the upper hand because they possessed money. But through Robert Owen and his disciples, and a growing public conscience, the spirit of reform was beginning to penetrate the minds of many men.

As a result of the strikes thousands of men, women and children were unemployed and starving on the pay they received from the benefit societies. Invariably they were forced to go back to work on whatever terms their employers handed out to them, so the strikes turned out to be fruitless. The year 1825 which had promised so well for employers and employees alike ended in financial failure for everyone.

Reluctantly, Parliament was forced to take action to try to sort out the situation and keep the peace. The Tories set up a second Select Committee on the same lines as that which had presented the workers' claims to Parliament a year earlier. But this time the members were picked by Tory ministers and Joseph Hume was the only true representative of the workers. After long discussions the Committee retired without producing a constructive plan. Parliament had repealed the Combination Acts and it was too dangerous for any political party to grant freedom of speech to a militant working class and then take it away.

Also there were changes in government thinking since the days of William Pitt. In 1822, Sir Robert Peel, a less aristocratic and more liberal Tory, had become Home Secretary, and his work was mainly concerned with domestic affairs.

Peel had working-class grandparents. His grandfather had been a calico printer, then a cotton spinner, who went into the textile business and made a great deal of money. Robert's father

Sir Robert Peel

carried on the firm, employed 15,000 workers and ran his factories on the then usual abominable lines. After receiving a baronetcy he turned to politics and his son, after Harrow and Oxford, followed in his footsteps. As Home Secretary Robert Peel worked for a more humane deal for the working class. He abolished the death penalty for a hundred minor crimes, such as stealing a pig, and put forward a plea for fair trials in the courts for all people. Perhaps his most lasting achievement was the foundation of an efficient police force which he recruited and put into action. Hitherto troops armed with swords and guns had been sent to trouble spots. Now the civil police in their blue uniforms and top hats went in armed with truncheons to restore order. The people felt safer and they were thankful. They liked the police and called them 'bobbies' (a name which still exists) as a token of gratitude to Robert Peel.

But the strikes continued and an acute industrial depression settled over Britain. Workers formed a Trade Union in many industries, but they discovered that when it came to resisting a pay reduction during a depression, these official Unions were no more powerful than the unofficial ones they had formed previously.

As Sidney and Beatrice Webb have pointed out, there is a great difference between a Trade Union and a Trades Union: 'A Trade Union is a combination of members of one trade; a Trades Union is a combination of different trades.'

The early labour leaders realized that they must negotiate from strength instead of desperation; and that in order to present a united front members of the same trade in different towns should combine for mutual support. But in the 1820s they did not have an organization powerful enough to confront the heads of industry with a winning plan.

Beside the labour disturbances Britain was seething with political unrest. Led by crusading radicals like Orator Hunt and William Cobbett the people clamoured for a parliamentary reform which would grant every man a chance to elect an MP of his choice.

The Whigs who were seeking to end the long Tory rule took sides with the protesting masses. They attacked the system by which only one Englishman in five had the right to vote because he happened to have money or property, and the other four were too poor to be placed on the electoral list. The militant Whigs also exposed the long-standing scandal of the 'rotten boroughs'. These seats were never really contested in a general election, but handed out by rich Whig and Tory political families to men who agreed to vote as they were told. These bogus MPs were not interested in the opinions of their constituents because they knew they held no political power.

The parliamentary reformers stressed the fact that no worker was able to vote for an MP who would represent working-class interests. But little by little life was changing. Working people were learning to read and write. If they could not make out for themselves the inflammatory pamphlets that the agitators circulated in the factories they could probably find a mate who would tell them what it was all about. Passions ran so high and the nation was so fiercely divided on parliamentary reform that it might easily have ended in civil war.

Events piled up to a crisis. In January 1828 the Duke of Wellington became Prime Minister of a Tory government. He had proved himself to be a magnificent commander on the field of battle, but he was a most unpopular premier. He was totally out of touch with the feeling of the country, rigidly conservative and opposed to any form of change. On the anniversary of the Battle of Waterloo crowds hooted at him in the streets and threw stones at his windows. At a state opening of Parliament in 1831 he declared himself opposed to any kind of parliamentary reform. A storm of national rage swept the Tories out of office.

Six months later, on 22 May 1832, the Reform Bill was carried through Parliament by Lord Charles Grey, a most far-sighted and talented Whig politician. He entered politics as a very young man and from the outset favoured parliamentary reform. But he was a Whig and the Tories were in power. For years he tried to build up an active opposition until he saw that it was impossible to convert the older members of the Whig party to modern policies. So he withdrew from active politics and left the struggle to the radical reformers.

Charles Grey retired to his house in Northumberland where he had a magnificent library, a loving wife and fifteen children. But he promised the Whig party that he would come back if he was needed. When the Tories collapsed he responded to popular appeal and returned to carry through the Reform Bill. He placed the Whigs in the forefront of the reform movement, and they remained the most stable and popular government for a generation to come.

The campaign for parliamentary reform had a profound effect

on British life outside the sphere of politics, for it drew the middle and lower classes together. They already had a bond in their religion because most of them were members of Wesleyan or other nonconformist sects, whereas the ruling class was Anglican. The dissenters attended the same chapels whether they were rich or poor, and they faced the same discrimination. No matter how brilliant, their children were debarred from Oxford and Cambridge and a number of professions. Unconsciously a certain sympathy and understanding grew up between the two classes which helped to bridge a gulf in labour relations in the future.

9 The Birth and Death of a Union

In 1834 labour leaders followed up their policy of strength through unity and formed the Grand National Consolidated Trades Union. It was sponsored by Robert Owen, the industrialist and reformer who at this period exerted immense influence on working people. The Grand Union was an exciting venture for it seemed to open up a way for every worker to take part in an immense national movement towards a better life. It aimed to give them a place in the particular Union that represented their own trade, whether they were builders, potters, shoemakers, farm hands, miners or skilled artisans; and an opportunity to present their wage demands without the disadvantages and dangers of a strike. The Grand Union caught on in a big way. After a few weeks of existence the organizers had enrolled half a million members, including factory workers, farm labourers and women in many trades who had never had any recognition or a chance to express themselves before, though they worked just as hard as the men.

The founders of the Grand Union hoped to teach the great mass of uninformed workers how to use their growing power to the best advantage and how, in a perfectly legal way, to sell their skills for what they were worth. It was planned as a peaceable, well-disciplined body, with its members contributing to a central fund which would be used for sickness benefit and to tide them over bad times. Almost every industry set up a branch with high hopes for the future. It was the first national Trades Union and it was large enough to put the fear of working-class domination into the minds of factory owners, shopkeepers, farmers and other employers of labour.

The Tolpuddle Martyrs were the first and most famous victims of a calculated attack on the Grand Union. In fact the six unfortunate farm labourers had a very fleeting connection with it for when they wanted to set up a little village Union of their own, they merely sought advice from the Grand Union headquarters. Two delegates visited Tolpuddle and the villagers then formed The Friendly Society of Agricultural Labourers. They did not try to keep their small society secret, for the Combination Acts had been repealed and as they were plotting no evil they thought they had nothing to fear.

As knowledge of their trial and conviction for conspiracy spread through Britain, a wave, first of amazement and then of indignation, swept the country. Members of Parliament received petitions signed by 80,000 constituents pleading for a reprieve for the six men. But the ruling Tories had not tried to interfere with the verdict and by the time the petitions came in the 'conspirators' had already sailed for Australia. They were all decent God-fearing country people – two of them were Methodist preachers – and their treatment was outrageous.

Once they landed in Australia they were either committed to hard labour, making roads through the wilderness chained to hardened criminals, thieves or murderers; or sent off to isolated farms where they were housed and fed no better than the animals.

The Grand Union took up their case and arranged a mass demonstration to ask the king for a royal pardon. Led by Robert Owen and the Reverend Arthur Wade, a Doctor of Divinity, about 40,000 people marched in perfect order through the streets of London to Whitehall. Wesleyans and Anglicans, members of Trade Unions and ordinary people who resented injustice and felt that their own freedom was threatened, took part in the march.

The local branch of the National Union of Agricultural Workers still
commemorates the events at Tolpuddle with annual rallies in the village

66

The pardon was granted in 1836, but communications were so slow in those days and the whereabouts of the six prisoners so remote that they returned only in 1838, after four years of extreme misery and separation from their families. It is sad that they could not live long enough to realize the contribution they had made to British working-class liberty. People in every walk of life were aware of the gross injustice and alerted to the brute force of the law. It was probably the last time in the legal history of Britain that a group of men of stainless character were punished for a crime they had never even thought of committing.

Unfortunately the Grand Union failed to fulfil its great promise. The Trades Unions were inexperienced and they lacked talented leadership. Strikes broke out once more, and funds ran out. The workers became disillusioned, membership diminished and in a few years it was disbanded.

In 1838 a band of working-class leaders launched their first purely political movement. It was known as Chartism from the original statement of their aims entitled The People's Charter. The Chartists made six separate points, all designed to give the working man the vote. Though the Reform Bill had abolished the rotten boroughs, the financial qualifications still deprived the workers of the right to vote, and they were no nearer to the ballot box than they had been before.

The Chartist doctrine of universal suffrage attracted a large and enthusiastic following. Chartist speakers toured the factory towns, holding meetings and distributing pamphlets. The Whig ministers did not try to suppress them, but they refused to take them seriously. Confronted by official indifference, the Chartists were deflated and frustrated. They lost the sense of united purpose which had inspired The People's Charter and serious dissension divided their leadership. Their council meetings were stormy and pointless because the members could never agree on a policy. Some favoured gaining the vote through official channels, even though they were narrow and difficult to navigate. Others were more impatient, and put their trust in organized riots and threats of violence, hoping by these revolutionary means to win their democratic ends.

In the early 1840s the British economy climbed out of the deep depression that had lasted for over fifteen years. Business began to prosper once more, trade revived and consequently there was more money around. Proprietors of businesses and farms could afford to be more generous and labour relations improved. Anyway the workers were growing weary of revolt. They were beginning to see that with their present tactics they were fighting a losing battle. 'Slum priests' drawn from nonconformist sects were moving into the factory areas, bringing spiritual comfort and sage counsel. People who had been utterly desperate began to hope that somehow, somewhere, there must be a better way of advancement than violence.

The Trade Unions were less aggressive in their approach to their employers, and some employers saw the writing on the wall and were prepared to negotiate with their workers for reasonable terms of service. They had all had a bad time and they welcomed the possibility of a truce in class warfare. This was only the beginning, but it was a symptom of the times.

Chartism had had its day. It had little to offer either revolutionaries or reformists and it died a natural death.

A new stage in industrial relations was about to begin.

10 Masters Versus Men

The first generation of Trade Union leaders who emerged after the repeal of the Combination Acts had resorted to threats and strikes, mainly because they considered that this was the only way to defeat their employers. They were inexperienced men, inspired by rash hopes of a swift victory. When they came up against the law, as they frequently did, they had no experienced lawyer to defend them, and if their wages were cut, as they often were, they had no one with enough knowledge of finance and business to tell them why it had happened.

Around 1850 a second generation of leaders took over from the Trades Union pioneers. Partly because business was booming and wages comparatively good, and partly because the workers had never scored a success by striking, these men sought other ways to better the lot of their members. As education increased they began to see the need for full-time officials, specially trained in Trade Union work, whom they could consult before going into action. These professional negotiators would be selected from among the workers for their ability, and paid according to the funds available to the particular Union that they worked for.

Above all the miners had need of good counsel. They were at a great disadvantage because they were tied to the system of yearly hiring; and they were also employed on the 'truck system'. This meant that instead of getting all their wages in cash, they received part of them in food coupons which they could use only at their employer's shop. Therefore they were compelled to stay at work in order to use up their earnings. This was an old-established custom and it provided them with food at reasonable prices, but deprived them of any possible independence. They were more backward than most other industries in Union organization, but during the 1840s miners from Northumberland and Durham, Lancashire and Yorkshire and Ireland formed an important association which they called the Miners' Society of Great Britain.

At this time the Masters and Servants Act was still in force and it was blatantly unjust, a handle for every employer to turn for his own ends. Briefly, it ruled that if a worker, for any reason whatsoever, wanted to stop work or change his or her job, it was a criminal offence punishable by imprisonment. If, however, an employer decided to lay off any number of his employees they had no redress, while he was able to sue for damages if they went on strike. No miner stood the slightest chance of acquittal in a court of law until some member of the Association saw that what was needed was an able legal adviser with labour sympathies.

It was not a job that many people wanted, for every case was going to be a tough fight against magistrates prejudiced in favour of the employers. The Association was lucky to find William Roberts, a tough and talented solicitor who specialized in mining problems. He put his immense energy to the work and made a great name for himself in the mining world. Soon he was taking on all the Trade Union cases and the magistrates found themselves dealing with a real expert. The masters no longer sailed through the cases they brought against their men with victory as a foregone conclusion. They had to fight and sometimes they lost. William Roberts was as astute as his opponents, and his interpretation of the law proved to be a formidable barrier to injustice. Employers were less inclined to take their employees to court for an expensive trial they were not certain to win.

William Roberts

This was a success story, but a hard struggle lay ahead. In 1844 the Durham miners embarked on a disastrous strike which not only failed to gain them any advantage, but also destroyed the Miners' Society of Great Britain.

It was replaced by twin organizations, both very carefully planned so as to avoid the mistakes of former Unions. One was the National Association of United Trades for the Protection of Labour, the main duty of which was to deal with disputes between masters and men and stimulate interest in the welfare of labour in the House of Commons. The second was the National United Trades Association for the Employment of Labour, the duty of which was to collect money to provide for workers who were on strike, provided that the aim was approved by both bodies. The contribution was fixed at two-pence out of every pound of the weekly wage packet, which for most workers was no more than £1 or £2. Many trades welcomed the new venture and joined the Association: carpenters and joiners, boot and shoe-makers, potters, the Scottish miners,

Mechanic's Magazine,
Museum, Register, Journal, & Gazette.

" States and kingdoms that aspire to greatness, must be very careful that their nobles and gentry increase not too much ; otherwise the common people will be dispirited, reduced to an abject state, and become little better than slaves to the nobility."   *Lord Bacon*

No. 7.]   SATURDAY, OCTOBER 11, 1823.   [Price 3*d.*

FIRST STEAM-BOAT.

ALTHOUGH it is only of late years that steam has been extensively applied to the propelling of vessels on water, yet a knowledge of its capabilities for this purpose is of old date. As far back as the 21st of December, 1736, Mr. Jonathan Hulls took out a patent for " A new invented Machine for carrying Vessels or Ships out of, or into, any Harbour, Port, or River, against Wind and Tide, or in a Calm ;" and in the following year, he published a pamphlet at London, which is now extremely rare, detailing at length the nature of his invention. Mr. Hulls' " new invented machine," as we shall presently show, was nothing else than a tow-boat moved by steam.

In the introduction to his pamph-let, Mr. H. prophetically remarks, " There is one great hardship lies too commonly upon those who propose to advance some new though useful scheme for the public benefit, the world abounding more in rash censure than in a candid and unprejudiced estimation of things ; if a person does not answer their expectation in every point, instead of friendly treatment for good intentions, he too often meets with ridicule and contempt." We are willing to think, that there is less of this ungenerous feeling to be met with now-a-days than formerly ; and yet even at the present time how many are the projects of genius for the benefit of mankind, which lie, thrown aside, neglected and contemned ? How can

An early edition of the *Mechanic's Magazine*

cordwainers, tailors, boiler-makers and masons all signed on. But once more the Associations foundered on a wave of trade depression, and for lack of centralized leadership.

Meanwhile many trades began to publish journals dealing with trade interests and trade politics. Among them were the *Potter's Examiner*, the *Mechanic's Magazine*, the *Bookbinder's Trade Circular* and the *Flint Glass Maker's Magazine*. Their aim was to hand out useful information and their tone was moderate. Many of them specifically advised against strikes as a means of improving the workers' position, and they urged the workers to study industrial problems.

With this new-found knowledge the workers in one trade after another began to realize the many complications of running their own Trade Union branches. At first it seemed easy to appoint one willing worker to organize the office, handle the correspondence, work out the accounts, allocate the payment of funds and keep the peace among the members. But it turned out that most workers, however industrious and enthusiastic, did not have the training or the experience to do the job.

Little by little a new brand of salaried officials appeared, dedicated workers who regarded Trade Union management as a career. Most of them aimed to draw their own local branches into a network of national power. Prominent among the growing Unions was the Journeymen Steam-Engine and Machine Makers and Millwrights Society which eventually became the Amalgamated Society of Engineers and has played a leading role in Trade Union history ever since. In 1851 it moved its headquarters to London, and far exceeded any other Trade Union in wealth and size of membership – largely because its members were all skilled workers and relatively well paid.

In the following year the members of the Amalgamated Society came into conflict with their employers. They proposed to abolish the state of perpetual overtime, and the custom of piece-work rates instead of a regular salary. The employers re-

The 1858 dispute was a major battle between employers and workers. These demonstrators, with banner defiantly calling for an eight-hour day, met to commemorate its third anniversary.

plied by a complete lock-out of the engineering trade. On 1 January 1852 they closed every engineering factory. The struggle continued for three months and aroused intense feeling throughout the country. The engineers won widespread sympathy and received considerable contributions from outside donors. But by the end of March the workers had to give in, and in order to get their jobs back they were forced to sign 'the document', a promise to abandon the Union. In fact, because they were obliged to accept 'the document' or starve, they did not regard the promise as honourable or binding. So they went back to work and kept up their Trade Union membership just the same. Far from breaking up the Trade Union movement the defeat of the engineers strengthened it. Many smaller Unions studied the engineers' Constitution and adopted it as the basis of their own Codes.

A brief period of peace settled over the Trade Union world. Both employers and employees brooded over the situation and conferred behind closed doors. In 1858 a Joint Committee of Carpenters, Masons and Bricklayers presented a carefully calculated proposal to the master builders for the ten-hour day to be reduced by one hour and suggested that future building con-

74

tracts should be calculated on this basis. The employers abruptly refused. All conciliation broke down; every master builder employing more than fifty men closed down his business and 24,000 men were thrown out of work.

The employers were adamant. Despite the growing moderation which had developed within Trade Union circles, the employers refused to discuss the situation. They clearly showed that they had not advanced with the times and they refused to make any concessions. Resolved to crush the Trades Unions once and for all they waved 'the document' in the face of would-be mediators.

The builders had loyal allies and men of many trades took up the struggle. Subscriptions flowed in from such diverse Societies as the Pianoforte Makers, the Flint Glass Makers and the Yorkshire miners. The Amalgamated Engineers sent three donations of £1,000 each. This was outright war between Capital and Labour. At the end of six months the employers agreed to scrap 'the document', but they refused to grant any other claims.

Out of the struggle the Carpenters' Union was born, and Robert Applegarth, secretary of the Sheffield branch, rose from the ranks of Trade Union leaders to a position of national authority. He possessed all the qualities that the new Trade Union spirit was seeking, and he inspired confidence, respect and recognition from many people who had hitherto opposed the labour movement.

11   'A Congress of our Own'

In 1968 the Trades Union Congress, commonly known today as the TUC, held centenary celebrations and published a well documented and beautifully illustrated book, summarizing the accomplishment of the whole Trades Union movement since the foundation of the Congress in 1868. It is a sensational record of both triumphant and troubled times, for the TUC has survived two world wars, the Great Depression of the early 1930s, the break-up of the British Empire and the onset of the nuclear age. The members have taken part in the steady improvement of social conditions in Britain and the establishment of the Labour party in the forefront of political power.

We have moved far and fast. In 1868 there were no motor cars on the roads; in 1968 men were exploring outer space and had already landed on the moon. In 1868 a labourer took a month to accomplish what the modern bulldozer does in a day. In 1868 two thirds of the British people could neither read nor write; by 1968 every British child had the right of free education from the age of five to fifteen. In 1868 if people were poor and ill they were cared for in miserable conditions and their chances of recovery were slim; in 1968 every sick person was entitled to treatment under the National Health Service by the best doctors in the country. The Trades Unions not only weathered the sweeping changes, but took an important hand in bringing many of them about. The history of the TUC is inseparable from the history of the nation.

It seems that the actual Trades Union Congress came into

76

being almost by chance. In 1865, William Dronfield, a journeyman printer, was bitterly disappointed to discover that a paper he had delivered at a Social Science Congress was not mentioned in the report of the proceedings. It was evidently too radical in its approach to current problems, and unacceptable to the other delegates. Dronfield talked to Sam Nicholson, his friend and fellow-printer, who reacted instantly. 'Why not have a congress of our own?' he said.

These enterprising printers gathered a group of colleagues and sent out invitations for a congress at Manchester in June 1868, for the purpose of discussing Trade Union aims. Thirty-four delegates turned up, most of them from Trade Councils, organizations which had grown up at first in London and then in other industrial towns to advise the local Trade Union branches on their policy, and protect them from the hazards of criminal law. In the following year forty delegates, representing about a quarter of a million workers, attended the Trades Union Congress at Birmingham, and from this time onwards the TUC became an annual event.

In 1867 a second Parliamentary Reform Bill to give more working-class men a vote was passed through the House of Commons, largely because of the stern insistence and brilliant oratory of John Bright – a Liberal, a Quaker and an ardent defender of the rights of ordinary people. The Bill fell far short of the full suffrage that the workers demanded, but it did give the artisan householders in the towns the vote that they had been clamouring for; though it left the farm labourers and miners in exactly the same position they had been in before, discontented and underprivileged.

At the time of the first Trades Union Congress many members of various trades were restive and rebellious. They had set out to abolish the Masters and Servants Act, and certain militants among them were ready to resort to violence. They whipped up feeling against non-Union workers, and 'blacklegs' (men

77

who would not support strikes) because they considered them traitors to the cause of Trade Unionism. Violence flared up, especially in Sheffield, and the climax came when an unknown agitator blew up the house of a non-Union worker with a can of home-made gunpowder. The press wrote up this and the other incidents as the 'Sheffield outrages' and they were the talk of every town in the country.

The public demanded an inquiry into the structure and strength of the Trades Unions, and their effect on the nation as a whole. Simultaneously, the sober leaders of the Unions who denied all knowledge of the terrorist activity, asked for a government commission to examine the source of the 'outrages' and establish their own innocence.

Robert Applegarth, General Secretary of the Amalgamated Society of Carpenters, proved himself an outstanding witness in the long-drawn-out inquiry. He claimed that the Trades Unions should not be condemned for the acts of certain disorderly individuals and that Trade Union policy was utterly opposed to violence. By his evident honesty, his quiet modera-

John Bright

A view of the events in Sheffield
from *Punch*

tion and carefully considered arguments, he did a great deal to dispel government fear and distrust, and widen public knowledge of the aims of the Trade Union movement.

The leading Whigs were divided in opinion, but in the end they passed two Bills. The first gave the Trades Unions the legal standing that they demanded; but the second, the Criminal Law Amendment Act, ruled that members of trade societies were liable to criminal charges for any misdeed. This aroused a storm among Trade Unionists. They considered the second Bill an insult and an indignity. With one accord they protested furiously against a law which gave magistrates the power to charge Trade Union members with a criminal act, whereas similar conduct of a non-member could only be counted a civil misdemeanour.

The TUC placed its protest to the Act first on the Agenda at Nottingham in 1872, then at Leeds in 1873 and at Sheffield in 1874. In this way the Trades Unions kept their urgent demands in the public eye, and openly condemned any government which ignored the question.

The fight for the repeal of the Criminal Law Amendment Act racked the Trades Union world for four years, though the workers had found a fine advocate in Alexander Macdonald, the leader of the Scottish miners. He had gone to work in the mines at the age of eight and, fourteen years later, by sheer hard work and determination, had entered Glasgow University. When he graduated he turned his entire life to improving conditions in the mines and obtaining fair wages for the mining community.

By the Mines Act of 1842 the state had forbidden the employment of women and boys under the age of ten years. And according to the Mines Inspectorate Act of 1850 mine owners were compelled to provide safety measures to cut down the terrible toll of accidents. But improvements came slowly, the old abuses lingered, and there was still need for experienced supervision and guidance.

The Criminal Law Amendment Act hit the miners harder than workers in most other trades, for they were a tough lot with great grounds for complaint, always likely to get up against the law.

Alexander Macdonald made one representation after another and gathered a following among the more liberal Members of Parliament to support his cause. A general election was looming and it was clear that no artisan who had recently got the vote would cast it for any party in favour of the hated Act. But the Whigs did not take warning, and it probably cost them the election. The Tories promised to meet Trade Union demands and won a sweeping victory. At the same time Alexander Macdonald and a working miner, Thomas Burt, were elected as the first working-class Members of Parliament. There was then no Labour party so they stood as Liberals and were known, with the other workers who were subsequently elected, as 'Lib–Labs'. In 1875 the Tories repealed the Criminal Law Amendment Act, and replaced it by the Employer and Workmen Act which gave Trade Unionists the same rights as other citizens.

In 1837 Queen Victoria had come to the throne at the age of eighteen. She ruled for sixty-four years, the longest reign in English history, and there was during her era growing recognition of the right of the working people to a fair share of the prevailing prosperity.

In 1846 the Corn Laws were abolished and the price of bread dropped. In 1851 the British held the Great Exhibition in London's Hyde Park to demonstrate to the world at large their undisputed industrial supremacy. It was perhaps unfortunate that most of the people who came to marvel and exclaim did not also visit the slum districts of the factory towns which produced the magnificent exhibits.

But little by little reforms crept in. Joseph Chamberlain, the man who led the way in slum clearance, was a free-thinking Whig, a businessman and a nonconformist. He favoured freedom of worship, freedom of speech and freedom from want for

Alexander Macdonald   Joseph Chamberlain

all people, not because he had suffered from poverty himself like
so many other reformers, but because he believed this was their
right.

When he became Mayor of Birmingham he transformed the
city and set an example of town planning that influenced every
other factory area in Britain. He saw the degrading effect of dirt
and overcrowding, tore down the squalid tenements, let light
into the slums, and laid on gas, water and sanitation. As a result
the health and happiness of the people increased and crime
diminished.

1871 was an important year for English education because
free state primary schools were founded which eventually provided teaching for every child; and Oxford and Cambridge over-
came their prejudices and opened their doors to students of
every religious denomination. In 1875 Parliament brought in
a law to end the cruel custom of sweeps sending little boys up
suffocating, soot-caked chimneys to do their work; and in 1884
the Society for the Prevention of Cruelty to Children was
founded.

Annie Besant

Girls at work in the
Bryant and May factory

Up till now it had been the skilled workers who had been demanding their rights and claiming a position in industry to which their skills entitled them. Now the unskilled workers, who had formerly suffered in silence, began to demand some recognition of the work they were doing. The end of the century was marked by three strikes. Six hundred London match girls working for the firm of Bryant and May rebelled against their miserable lives. They were inspired by a writer named Annie Besant who published an article on their plight in a socialist journal which she edited. She was a member of the Fabian Society, a small high-powered socialist group of intellectuals like Bernard Shaw and Sidney and Beatrice Webb, who were working for social equality. When the match girls went on strike people were shocked by their pathetic state. They were half-starved and clad in rags, and their employers raised their wages to pacify public protest.

Shortly afterwards the gas workers of a London suburb approached their employers with a reasonable request for three eight-hour shifts a day instead of two twelve-hour shifts, and won their point.

In 1889 the London dockers came out on strike. They had plenty of grievances, for they were paid fourpence or fivepence an hour, a pittance even in those days, and in addition most of them could only get casual labour depending on the state of trade and the size of the cargoes. When they were out of work they hung around the docks, and no one seemed to care if their families lived or died.

They enlisted the help of two socialist-minded engineers, John Burns and Tom Mann, and of Ben Tillett, an ardent defender of working-class rights. Tillett organized the dockers and voiced their claims. They demanded sixpence an hour, the 'dockers' tanner', and an end to piece-work. The great port of London came to a standstill, while the dockers wound their way in sullen and silent procession through the streets of the city, bearing banners flaunting socialist slogans, and poles topped by stinking

The conference held to settle the great docks strike.
Tillett and Burns (with beard) are in the foreground

83

fish heads and rotten onions as symbols of their current diet. Under Tillett's direction there was no violence, and at night they returned to their dockside hovels.

With the patient help of Cardinal Manning, a Roman Catholic priest concerned for the welfare of the Irish dockers, Tillett strove for a just settlement. Suddenly help came from an unexpected source. Dockers in Australia, much better off than their British brothers, sent them handsome donations and they were able to hold out until the employers granted almost all their demands.

The outcome of these strikes was a sign of the times. The days were past when masters silenced their servants' protests, secure in the knowledge that the ruling class favoured the wealthy and ignored working-class suffering. Collective bargaining had become the law of the land. Reforms took place not through the outright class warfare that Karl Marx and his disciples had predicted but through a slowly awakening social conscience, the inspired leadership of certain outstanding politicians and the dogged determination of the Trades Unions to defeat oppression.

12 Britain Goes to War

With the twentieth century a new political party was born. The movement for independent labour representation in the House of Commons, free from a Liberal label, was started by Keir Hardie, a Scottish miner, who worked his way into political prominence from a very humble and hard-working background. He was born in a one-room cottage in Lanarkshire in 1856. By the age of seven he was working in a tavern, but he lost his job because he was late for work. He would not explain to his master that he had been up all night looking after a sick brother. At twelve he went into the mines, and would probably have started sooner but for the recent Bill prohibiting women and very young boys on the coal face. He took an interest in politics at an early age, starting out as a Liberal and soon turning socialist.

He felt very strongly the need for a united Labour party and approached the TUC. He persuaded them, after some hesitation, to arrange a meeting between their Parliamentary Committee, the Trade Union officials and independent socialist societies. It took place in London on 27 February 1900 which is generally regarded as the founding date of the Labour party. Keir Hardie was a forceful and fiery character and a colourful speaker. He gave his listeners a vision and a sense of purpose. He was popular with the workers, but at times the TUC found him obstinate and troublesome to handle, because he was so set on a separate role for Labour that he enraged the Parliamentary Committee and the Lib–Labs.

Many Trade Union leaders felt that it would be better to con-

A Keir Hardie election poster

tinue to deal with the House of Commons through the existing channels; and they were reluctant to face up to the expense of financing Labour candidates in a general election and then giving them a fixed salary. As they would all be working men they would need to earn a living and in those days the state did not pay its Members of Parliament anything at all. Keir Hardie was disappointed at the general lack of enthusiasm, but three large Unions agreed to join the Labour party: the Amalgamated Society of Railway Servants, who had a lot to gain from direct representation in Parliament, the Printers who had always been adventurous and outspoken in their views, and the Shoemakers. In addition, a number of small Unions of unskilled workers, labourers and shop assistants, gave their support, hoping to improve their status.

Six months later the new Labour party fought its first election. Out of fourteen candidates only Keir Hardie and Richard Bell, the Secretary of the Railway Servants, won seats. But the situation changed rapidly. The textile workers and the engineers de-

86

cided that the movement was worthwhile and increased the membership. After three years the Unions agreed on a compulsory levy so that they would have money to pay Labour MPs.

The next general election followed in 1906. The Conservatives were in a bad way, torn apart by the questions of free trade and Home Rule for Ireland. When the votes were counted fifty-four working-class candidates had been elected, twenty-nine members of the Independent Labour party and the rest Lib–Labs. In the ensuing years there was considerable dissension in Labour circles. Many Trade Unionists resented the compulsory levy to the Labour party, whilst a number of those belonging to Unions not affiliated to the Labour party resented their enforced loyalty to the Liberals.

In 1911 David Lloyd George, a Welsh Nationalist and a radical Liberal, was Chancellor of the Exchequer. He passed a National Insurance Bill through the House of Commons which greatly improved the condition of the British working class by social insurance and followed it with an Unemployment Insurance Bill, both entirely new ventures in British politics. At first there was a storm of protest from other classes which gradually died down as the benefits became obvious. In this same year Parliament agreed to pay all MPs a salary of £400 a year which rose by stages to £3,250 in 1964 and is now £6,062.

The Labour party was all the time consolidating its position. The Trades Unions formed the Labour Representation Committee as their branch of the new Labour movement, and Ramsay MacDonald, a comparatively recent recruit to socialism, represented them in the House of Commons. Local councils set up offices in many constituencies with branch secretaries who collected money and organized election campaigns. Keir Hardie was aging rapidly and took far less part in public affairs, but he has held an honoured position as a pioneer in the Labour movement ever since.

Already Ernest Bevin, the man who rose to the most powerful

position ever held by a British working-class politician, had entered the Trade Union world.

He was born in 1881 in the little Somerset village of Winsford. His mother, Diana Tudball, married a local labourer and had seven children, first a girl and then six boys, of whom Ernest was the youngest. She moved with her husband and the eldest children to South Wales where he was looking for work. It is not known what happened, but she returned to Winsford and described herself as a widow. When Ernest was born she registered his birth leaving a blank where his father's name should have been.

The family was terribly poor and as soon as the children were old enough they went out to work. Diana Bevin hired herself out as a domestic help and sometimes as a midwife to keep her family in the bare necessities of life. She got them the best available education in the village school and Ernest attended the Wesleyan Sunday School at a very early age. His mother died when he was eight, and he went to live with his sister and her

The young Ernest Bevin

husband who worked on the railways. He continued his schooling until the age of eleven. He then found work as an odd-job boy on a neighbouring farm. As he was the only member of the household who could read and write he spent his evenings giving the family the news from the Bristol papers, so he got some idea of city life. When he was thirteen he went to Bristol and got a job working twelve hours a day, six days a week, in a bakery where one of his brothers was learning to be a pastrycook. During the next few years he changed jobs very often, working on the tramways, as a waiter and a van boy. In 1901, at the age of twenty, he went to work as a carter for a firm of mineral-water manufacturers, where he drove a horse and wagon, delivering soft drinks. He signed on for a year, but he liked the job and so stayed for five. The life suited him well, for he was out of doors and independent. He enjoyed driving through the Bristol streets, choosing his own way, keeping his own timetable, and getting to know his customers.

Ernest Bevin kept up his habit of chapel going and joined a Baptist Mission as a Sunday School teacher. Nonconformist teaching contributed enormously to Trade Unionism. It gave young men religious faith and moral standards, and an opportunity to speak in public. James Moffat Logan, a Bristol Baptist minister, crammed his chapel with men of different faiths and totally conflicting ideas. And they all had a chance to air their opinions on every subject, test their beliefs in open debate and develop the art of oratory in a very competitive way. Bevin took an active part, and though later he turned from religion to socialism he never lost the human touch learned in his chapel days.

As he drove his wagon through the Bristol slums and the prosperous middle-class areas he began to wonder if it was right to accept a social system creating such inequality. He read everything he could lay his hands on and instead of going to chapel he joined the Right-to-Work Committee, a welfare society.

1908 was a bad year for Bristol and Bevin was in the thick of it. By December 6,000 men were out of work and their dependants were cold and starving. He visited London for the first time to put the situation to the National Headquarters of the Right-to-Work Committee, and he fought and lost an election for a seat on the city council. He was angry and dejected, and it was lucky that he was already married to Florence Townley, a Bristol girl, who made him a fine partner and gave him a happy home for the rest of his life.

In 1910 a strike broke out in the Bristol docks, and the carters who carried goods to the ships suffered with the rest. Bevin persuaded them to join the Dock, Wharf, Riverside and General Workers' Union for their own protection and became their first chairman. He was twenty-nine years old and a Trade Union member for the first time in his life. He succeeded in negotiating an agreement with the employers which gave the dockers and the carters better working terms than they had ever had before. He began to feel his power and plot his future. He worked with Ben Tillett, well known for his part in the London dock strike of 1889, and the most stirring orator in the country. He travelled to South Wales where relations between the miners and the owners were bitter and explosive, using all his powers of conciliation to bring the two sides together and avert the tragedy of open violence. He was deeply involved in Trade Union work in the summer of 1914 when the First World War broke out with startling suddenness, and the British people were drawn into the forefront of hostilities.

Not only the Labour party, which was hemmed in by its own problems, but most other people in Britain were almost unaware of the mounting threat of war. They were dimly conscious of the armaments race between Britain and Germany, then ruled by the Kaiser Wilhelm II. But the actual outbreak of war came like a thunderclap.

In June 1914 the heir to the Austrian throne was assassinated by a political fanatic in the Balkan state of Serbia, and Austria, encouraged by Germany, declared war to avenge his murder. In England the assassination seemed very far away. But the system of European alliances was extremely complicated. Russia and France had a secret defence pact against German aggression and Britain had guaranteed the little country of Belgium against German attack. The Kaiser was well prepared for war and determined to dominate Europe. He decided to conquer France by a swift blow and then turn on Russia. The quickest route to Paris lay through Belgium, so he tore up the pact with Britain, the famous 'scrap of paper', and sent a large army across the Belgian frontier. By August Britain, France and Russia had mobilized their forces and Europe was aflame with war.

The British Labour movement was divided. All over the country impassioned speakers were calling on the people to refuse to fight. Ramsay MacDonald, a confirmed pacifist, resigned the leadership of the Labour party. Keir Hardie appealed to the Socialist International, which had recently been formed to unite the labour movements of many countries, to instruct their workers to lay down their tools and call a general strike which would make war impossible. The British Trades Unions discarded the idea as unpatriotic and impractical. Keir Hardie died in 1915 at the age of fifty-nine, broken-hearted at the split in the Labour party, for many workers joined the large body of British people who, despite the fact that they hated bloodshed, were ready to do everything within their power to defeat the enemy and defend their homeland.

Ernest Bevin was also opposed to the war; but when the government fulfilled its promise to Belgium he decided to support the decision.

13   The Unions Join Up

Ramsay MacDonald, true to his pacifist ideals, gave up his party leadership as a protest against the declaration of war and faced public criticism. Most Trade Unionists, however, responded to the call to arms. Men flocked to the colours from every industry, and they were replaced by workers from non-essential jobs and by a great many women.

In order to further the war effort Trade Union leaders agreed that there would be no strikes for the duration of hostilities, and, moreover, that they would not insist on the conditions of work that they had struggled to establish for so many years. This meant that they would not hold up production by limiting working hours, and that they would not exclude unskilled workers from certain specific jobs.

In return the government promised that after the war the workers would resume their former position in industry so that they would not be penalized for their patriotism. Members of the War Cabinet also promised that employers would not be permitted to make excess profits from war production at the expense of the workers; a pledge that they were not able to keep. With the urgent need for tanks and guns, ships and aircraft, munitions and every other kind of war material, it proved impossible to control the manufacturers and many of them made large fortunes. The workers observed the profiteering with anger and distaste, and it was remarkable that they did not call more strikes. Those that did occur were almost all unofficial and settled by compulsory government arbitration.

David Lloyd George

The British were ill-prepared for war on such a vast scale and it took time to speed up the assembly lines and gear the shipyards to the formidable task of keeping up with the U-boat sinkings. It soon became clear that workers in certain key jobs must not be released to join the armed forces because they were so badly needed on the home front. Foremost among them were the miners, engineers and railwaymen whose skills and experience were essential to war production. In January 1916 the government passed a Military Service Act conscripting for the services unmarried men between the ages of eighteen and forty-one. Five months later it became necessary to include married men of military age. Neither the government nor the TUC approved of this measure, but it was forced upon them because they had to reinforce the battered divisions fighting on the Western Front, and stem the tide of the German advance.

In December 1916 David Lloyd George became Prime Minister of a coalition government and took Tom Henderson, a prominent Trade Union leader, into his War Cabinet. He also appointed Trade Unionists as Ministers of Labour and of Pensions. For the first time the Unions represented the people at the very highest political level.

Early in the war shop stewards began to take an important part in the Trade Union world. Originally they were minor officials, chosen from the men in a particular workshop, and paid a small salary to see that their comrades kept up their agreed contributions to Union funds. At the same time they coped with trivial day-to-day factory problems. But, gradually, as the Unions grew larger and the war caused a considerable movement of manpower into the munitions industries, the full-time officials lost touch. The shop stewards were on the spot and they took over. They listened to the workers' grievances and handled their negotiations with the employers. Especially in the large engineering and shipbuilding workshops they became very influential indeed.

Ernest Bevin held no official government post during the war. Instead he did a magnificent job in his own field. Besides organizing the Dockers' Union he served on the Executive Committee of the Transport Workers' Federation which represented the interests of thirty different Unions, and had also formed a Triple Alliance with the miners and railwaymen. Having enrolled the seamen, the Thames watermen, the bargees, the dockers, the stevedores and the road service workers, the Federation represented the whole system of transport labour and took over their wartime problems. Very early on Bevin saw that unless Trade Union leaders could keep transport running smoothly and swiftly Britain had not a hope of winning the war.

Bevin was based in Bristol, but he travelled constantly to ports in South Wales and anywhere else where there was trouble. Frequently he returned to London to report back to Federation headquarters. He spent his days and nights negotiating pay claims, supervising conditions of work, solving transport difficulties and negotiating the handling of dangerous cargoes. He examined the workers' complaints and pacified the port authorities. He understood the men's point of view because he was one of them and never ceased to be proud of it. He wanted the best he could get both for them and for the country. But he always seemed to know the right moment to compromise. When he sensed that the employers were nearing the limit of their concessions he came to terms and persuaded the men first to accept them, and then to stand by them.

On the occasions when he considered the workers' claims unreasonable he told them so and tried to find another way around the deadlock. Over and over again he settled disputes and averted stoppages at a time when delay on the docks or the railways meant certain death for the soldiers, sailors and airmen in action.

By the spring of 1917 the French and British forces were hard pressed and the civilian population was suffering from food shortages. Merchant ships had been commandeered to carry troops and the U-boat blockade had caused heavy loss. There was no weakening of the determination to fight on, but there were times when defeat seemed perilously near. On 6 April the balance of power changed dramatically. Woodrow Wilson, President of the United States, declared war on Germany, and a whole new reservoir of manpower and materials, the wealth and will of a great nation, flowed across the Atlantic.

With renewed strength the Allies were able to face a serious setback on the Eastern Front, when Russian resistance to Germany collapsed. In the autumn of 1917 revolution broke out in Russia and her armies stopped fighting. The country was ruled by the Tsar Nicholas II, an absolute monarch, heir to a long line of imperial monarchs. Nicholas was well meaning, but totally out of touch with his people, most of whom were desperately poor. Many moderate Russians had been imploring him to form a coalition government to try to relieve the sufferings of the soldiers at the front, the peasants in the countryside and the workers in the towns. But Nicholas was not prepared to surrender his authority. The Russian troops had fought heroically but they were no match for the Germans. They were badly led and armed with outdated weapons, and the men were disheartened to hear that their families at home were starving. Morale was very low. Finally in March 1917 Nicholas agreed to abdicate, and a provisional government was set up to cope with the widespread chaos.

This was the moment that the socialist revolutionaries had been waiting for. Vladimir Ulyanov, better known by his conspirator's name of Lenin, was a fanatical disciple of Karl Marx. He had spent years studying Marx's writings and was fully convinced that the only way to reform society was by total revolution. Lenin came to power in Russia through underground propaganda and highly organized conspiracy. He called his followers first Bolsheviks and later Communists. The army was riddled with Bolshevik agents urging the troops to lay down their arms. Lenin did not consider it treacherous to undermine their fighting spirit, because he was sure that once revolution broke out in a single country it would spread like wildfire; national barriers would disappear and the workers of the world would unite in a universal Communist state. He was certain that the Germans would join the Communist ranks, not as conquerors but as comrades so it would not matter who had won the war.

Lenin applied for an armistice, but when most Russians heard the terms proposed by the Germans they were shocked and ashamed. Civil war broke out in Russia, but Lenin was not disturbed, for he shared Marx's conviction that social change could arise only as a result of violence and the destruction of the existing way of life. When the Russian armies stopped fighting the Germans turned their entire military force against the Allies on the Western Front.

Finally on 11 November 1918 the First World War came to an end. The Kaiser had fled to Holland and the German High Command surrendered. The following year the leaders of the victorious nations met in the gleaming Hall of Mirrors in the Palace of Versailles to draft a Peace Treaty. The terms were harsh: the German army was disbanded, her navy scuttled and she was forced to pay reparations for the damage done to other nations. Some politicians, particularly in the Labour party, considered them too oppressive, but the general aim in the aftermath of the war was to make it impossible for Germany ever to attack again.

There was great enthusiasm when Woodrow Wilson produced a plan for permanent peace through a League of Nations. To the war-weary nations it seemed an inspiration, for the leaders would meet together and settle their disputes by words instead of guns. It was an overwhelming blow to Wilson that though the European nations welcomed his plan the United States Congress refused to join the League. The Americans had been drawn into one war to save the world from German aggression and they were determined to keep out of foreign affairs in the future.

14 The Depths of Depression

As soon as the fighting ended the Labour party withdrew from the wartime coalition government. In December 1918, just a month after the Armistice was signed, Lloyd George dissolved Parliament and went to the country in what was called 'the khaki election'. Now that the years of hardship were ended, and the dreaded casualty lists a thing of the past, people began to look ahead with well-earned optimism. They were enthusiastic about Lloyd George's forecast that a new coalition government would provide a 'land fit for heroes'.

In 1918 the great Parliamentary Reform Bill was passed granting a vote to men over twenty-one and women over thirty. The only qualification they had to have was a fixed address. The results of 'the khaki election' were sensational. The Conservative–Liberal Coalition won 474 votes, the Labour party fifty-seven and the independent Liberals twenty-six. All but eight of the Labour MPs were nominated by the Trades Unions, which also paid their election expenses. Ramsay MacDonald and his fellow socialists were all defeated because of their pacifism.

The new government set out with high hopes because in the early post-war years trade was booming. Prices were high, customers demanded the goods that they had not been able to buy during the war, and when soldiers, sailors and airmen were demobilized they found jobs waiting for them. But in 1920 the boom broke, and it dawned on politicians and manufacturers alike that Britain no longer held the lead in world industry. The United States was mass-producing goods in up-to-date factories

A miner's wife entering a pawn shop during the 1921 strike

by means of modern techniques and shipping them across the Atlantic. British manufacturers responded by cutting their costs, lowering their prices, reducing their workers' wages and dismissing any who were not absolutely essential. It was a poor outlook.

By 1921 the number of unemployed had risen to 2 million. The Trade Union leaders were angry and resentful. Their members had worked hard and fought well to win the war with little reward; whereas many of their employers had made fortunes. The miners were particularly bitter as they had been nationalized for the war effort and were strongly opposed to going back to private ownership. A Royal Commission was set up to consider the whole situation. In its final report the Commission supported nationalization; but the government,

Ramsay MacDonald

swayed by the Conservative mine owners, turned it down flat. The miners struck, but they did not have the organization or the funds to back up their demands and they returned to work with a heavy wage cut. A dock strike was peacefully settled in the dockers' favour, mainly because of the practical evidence of Ernest Bevin who exhibited in court, for all to see, the limited amount of food a docker could afford to buy with his present wages.

In 1921 a General Council of the TUC had been formed to direct industrial action. It was an influential body, dedicated to defending the rights of Trade Union members and by no means always in accord with the policy of the Parliamentary Labour party. At a general election in 1924 the Labour party triumphantly increased its number of seats in Parliament from fifty-seven to 191, and took office for the first time with Ramsay MacDonald as Prime Minister. It did not have an overall majority, but with Liberal support it outnumbered the Conservatives.

This first Labour government was shortlived. It faced hard times at home and a complicated situation abroad. By this time a Communist government was firmly established in the Soviet Union. Most people in Britain were strongly opposed to this revolutionary regime. As the Labour party had always been sympathetic to socialist aims the government gave official recognition to the Soviet Union and proposed closer trade relations. The motion was heavily defeated in the House of Commons and a Conservative government took over with Stanley Baldwin as Prime Minister and Winston Churchill as Chancellor of the Exchequer.

They were confronted by a grim situation and once more the miners were in the forefront of the trouble. In 1924 the coal owners had agreed to a rise in wages, but in the following year Winston Churchill, in an attempt to set British finances in order, returned to the gold standard. This meant that the £ sterling fell into line with other currencies taking their value from the international price of gold bars. It raised the value of the £ to its pre-war level which was more than it was actually worth, and made it very expensive for other countries to buy British goods. Coal was a major export and the only way the mine owners could sell it at a profit was to reduce the price and also the miners' wages. The miners protested furiously and Baldwin offered them a temporary subsidy while a Royal Commission under Sir Herbert Samuel, a prominent Liberal statesman, considered the whole future of the mining industry. By the time the Royal Commission handed in its report recommending limited wage cuts feeling was running dangerously high. The miners coined the war cry 'Not a penny off the pay, not a second on the day,' and prepared to strike.

The General Council of the TUC set up a committee to direct strike action, and one by one the Unions pledged themselves to support the miners. On 4 May 1926 a million miners stopped work and on the following day, with the consent of the General Council, a million and a half men employed in the docks, transport, building, printing, the iron and steel industry, chemical works and many other Unions joined the General Strike. Buses, trams and railways stopped running, blast furnaces and power

A miners' band at Epsom Races in 1926

stations were as deserted as the pits. Newspaper offices closed down and cargoes remained in the holds. Life came to a standstill and people stood around in aimless groups, confused and uncertain what to do next. In a few days the government organized troops and police and collected volunteers to operate essential services. Students drove buses and a few trains, and food was delivered under armed escort. There was some violence, but no one was killed.

A week later Sir Herbert Samuel presented proposals to a Negotiating Committee of the General Council which he hoped would be acceptable to both sides. Unfortunately no leading miners sat on the Negotiating Committee and when they heard the terms second-hand they rejected them outright. The General Council was divided in its views. The Union leaders realized that they were not properly prepared for a long strike, and their funds would soon run out. They saw too that the miners had set their faces against any compromise whatsoever. So, on the

102

ninth day of the strike, they decided to accept the Samuel offer and order a return to work. It was a complete surrender, for they failed to get any assurance from the government of future consideration of their claims. The members of the Unions who had come out in sympathy were humiliated by the defeat, and the miners felt themselves deserted and betrayed. They stayed out on strike for another six months, until they were driven back to work by cold, hunger and despair. The mines were not nationalized and they were forced to accept conditions far worse than those contained in the Samuel Report.

The General Strike had a disastrous effect on the Unions. The men lost faith in their leaders and the membership dropped. The small Communist party which had been formed in Britain after the First World War cashed in on their weakness, circulated revolutionary propaganda among the factory workers and recruited about 12,000 members. It aimed to create unrest and

A food lorry with armed escort in 1926

rebellion throughout industry and followed the lines of Marxist doctrine dictated by Moscow. It happened too that, owing to the general unrest, men and women of moderate views began to talk the language of revolutionary violence. Intellectuals who had been content to be Liberals thought of joining the Communist party. It was beginning to find a place among political scientists, publishers and teachers, people who were in a position to influence public opinion.

In May 1929 Britain went to the polls and for the first time Labour won more seats than any other party. Unemployment had risen under the Conservatives and people hoped for better times through a change of leadership. Ramsay MacDonald became Prime Minister for the second time and was instantly plunged into grave financial difficulties. Government funds were drained by unemployment benefits, trade was bad and the country could not balance its budget.

A serious rift in policy appeared within the Parliamentary Labour party. Some Labour ministers, led by MacDonald, proposed to tackle the crisis by drastic economies: cutting down on government spending, including the social services, and restricting investment in industry. On the other hand, the Trades Unions, led by Ernest Bevin, advocated expansion and government-backed enterprise to recover lost markets and provide more jobs. The Trades Unions rejected MacDonald's leadership but he and some of his colleagues agreed to serve in a peacetime coalition government with Conservatives and Liberals. The Trades Unions regarded this as a betrayal of socialist solidarity. After many years of fighting for recognition as a united movement representing the working class, the Labour party was split.

In 1929 a severe financial depression struck the United States. The nation had seemed so powerful and prosperous, and wealth so widespread that the crash was almost unimaginable. Investors had been speculating wildly and suddenly their stocks and shares were almost worthless. Fortunes disappeared overnight,

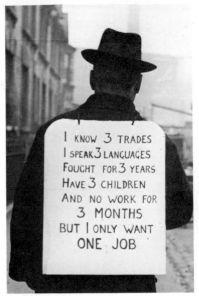

A poignant placard from the 1930s

Ellen Wilkinson leads the
Jarrow marchers

banks failed, businesses closed down for want of capital and schools for want of heating. People of every profession and trade were thrown out of work. Panic spread to Europe and the situation in Britain, where the national government was in power, went from bad to worse. Foreign financiers took fright and withdrew gold from London banks. All over the country the depressed areas grew larger and the queues at the Labour Exchanges longer. In the early 1930s more than $2\frac{1}{2}$ million workers were unemployed, their families living in hopeless misery on the 'dole', the meagre allowance paid by the government to keep them alive. The worst hit districts were the mines and the shipyards, lying idle because there were no orders for new vessels and little demand from overseas countries for coal. In the mining town of Crook in 1936, 71 per cent of the miners had not worked for five years and the school leavers had never worked at all.

Of the many protest meetings and hunger marches one of the

105

most famous set out in 1936 from Jarrow, a little town near New-castle in north-eastern England. The shipyards were closed and there was no alternative employment. Organized by the Jarrow Borough Council and led by their Labour MP Miss Ellen Wilkinson the workers marched 300 miles to Westminster in twenty-six days. They sang as they marched to keep up their spirits. The Jarrow March became a national affair, for all along the route they were greeted as crusaders in the common cause.

The national government did its best to stem the tide of indus-trial distress. The Trade Union leaders were almost powerless to help their comrades, for they were weakened by the legislation that followed the collapse of the General Strike and again by a crushing defeat for Labour in a recent general election. More-over, men who were out of work could not afford to pay Union subscriptions so they were very short of money, and it was obvious that in slump conditions no Union could win a strike.

Little by little Britain climbed out of the depression. It was a slow and painful process. The government increased income tax for wage earners and charged a surtax on private incomes, collected more duty on beer, cigarettes, petrol and enter-tainment. At the same time the Cabinet cut the salaries of its own ministers, judges, the armed forces, teachers, policemen and panel doctors. It was forced to reduce unemployment benefits, and it increased National Insurance contributions and built fewer roads. In the United States conditions were improving and the government granted Britain a loan of £80,000,000. As other nations surmounted the crisis they began to buy British goods once more and new inventions created new industries. Factories were built to manufacture synthetic fibres, plastics and chemi-cals; and a big business in processed foods provided new jobs.

But, by 1938, an even greater danger than idleness and poverty loomed large in Europe. Adolf Hitler and his Nazi fol-lowers were on the warpath in Germany.

15 Total War and the Trade Unions

The German people had been stunned by their defeat in the First World War. They had immense pride in their military might and until the end they had been confident of victory. The terms of the Versailles Treaty stripped them of power and they were no longer a great nation. In addition to the shame of surrender they had to face the collapse of their currency. At the end of the war the German mark had been valued at five pence; by 1923 it took thousands of marks to buy a loaf of bread and mil-

German inflation was so acute in the early 1920s that money taken for goods in this small provincial store overflowed the cash register

lions to pay a week's rent. People with savings lost them all and were destitute.

But the Germans are industrious and they went to work to rebuild their lives until in 1930 the great depression spread from the United States to Europe. In Germany millions of men and women were unemployed, starving and rebellious. At this time of deep despair Adolf Hitler began to address mass audiences, filling them with hatred of their conquerors and dreams of revenge.

Hitler was Austrian, a political agitator with no settled job, living in a home for tramps in a Vienna slum. He was a brilliant orator and he told the downcast Germans what they wanted to hear most. They were out of work and he promised them jobs if they would follow him. He hailed them as a master race and revived their pride and ambition. And he taught them to loathe the Jews, whom he blamed for the defeat and all the other German troubles. Hitler founded the National Socialist party, Nazi for short, and climbed to power through trickery and violence. In 1933 he took over the German government, and from then onwards he called himself the *Führer* (Leader) of the German people, and ruled as a supreme dictator.

The peace-loving statesmen of the world watched the rise of Hitler, at first with amazement and then with terror. Though Winston Churchill had repeatedly warned British leaders of the mounting threat of war, they did not take it seriously. They could not believe that the ranting Austrian upstart could become really dangerous. But when Hitler began to rearm the nation and marched troops into the Rhineland, a part of Germany which had been demilitarized under the Versailles Treaty, they could no longer ignore the Nazi menace.

In 1937, a year after the occupation of the Rhineland, Neville Chamberlain became Prime Minister of a Conservative government in Britain. He was the son of Joseph Chamberlain who had done so much to improve the conditions of working-class

Neville Chamberlain speaks on his return from Munich
in September 1938

people, and he had been brought up in an atmosphere of human kindness and social reform. He was a man of high ideals, totally unfitted to deal with a ruthless dictator. Nevertheless Chamberlain took upon himself the role of world peacemaker and flew to Germany three times to negotiate with the *Führer*. On each occasion Hitler made solemn promises of non-aggression and broke them as soon as it suited him.

In 1938 he occupied Austria, and the following year Czechoslovakia. He accomplished both conquests by intrigue and intimidation, first saturating the people with Nazi propaganda and then blotting out the skies with squadrons of dive-bombers and the countryside with armoured divisions. He did not need to fire a single shot since the free world looked on helplessly.

After the conquest of Austria and Czechoslovakia it was obvious that Poland, lying comparatively defenceless on Germany's eastern frontier, would be the next victim. Hoping to deter Hitler Britain and France declared that in case of Nazi attack they would go to Poland's aid. But it was far too late. Hitler had signed pacts with Benito Mussolini, Fascist dictator of Italy, and Joseph Stalin, Communist dictator of the Soviet Union. With these two powerful allies he was strong enough to go ahead with his plans. On 1 September 1939, Nazi forces crossed the Polish frontier, and two days later Britain and France declared war on Germany. It was impossible to send help to the Poles because Germany blocked the way. The Poles fought gallantly, but they were overcome by an avalanche of enemy fire and swift-moving tanks. In four weeks the war in Poland was ended.

An uneasy lull settled over Europe. Neither France nor Britain were prepared for total war. French generals put their trust in the Maginot Line, a massive string of frontier forts; and the British had fallen far behind Germany in armaments because they had clung too long to false hopes of peace. The two allied nations mobilized their forces as best they could while Hitler made ready for his next move. In April 1940 German forces stormed into Norway. British and French troops joined the Norwegian defenders, but it was a losing battle. The Germans held all the airfields, and on 8 May the Allies withdrew and the Norwegians laid down their arms.

The British people were humiliated and indignant. They held the government responsible for the defeat, and the Labour party, led by Clement Attlee, moved a vote of censure in the House of Commons. Neville Chamberlain resigned and King George VI invited Winston Churchill to form a national coalition government. The Labour party agreed to serve under his vigorous leadership and Labour members took office in the War Cabinet including Clement Attlee as Deputy Prime Minister and Ernest Bevin as Minister of Labour and National Service. This was an unexpected appointment, for Bevin at the age of fifty-nine had never even been a MP. But Churchill had recognized the value of his work, and he also foresaw the vital part that the Trade Unions would need to play in the war effort. He chose Ernest Bevin as the man who understood them better than anyone else.

On 10 May 1940, the same day that Churchill took over the leadership of the nation, Hitler launched his long-awaited offensive on the Western Front. Columns of tanks streamed into Belgium and Holland and, after a few days' fighting, other armoured divisions crossed the River Meuse and broke through the French defences. At the same time the *Luftwaffe* (German Air Force) sent wave after wave of dive-bombers to spread destruction and panic behind the lines. The Belgians and Dutch were powerless to resist the onslaught; Italy attacked France along the Mediterranean coast; and on 16 June the French government sued for an Armistice. Britain stood alone.

Churchill did not try to conceal the seriousness of the situation from the British people. In a speech which will be forever famous he admitted that he could offer them nothing but 'blood, toil, tears and sweat' until final victory.

Conscription for the armed forces was introduced early in the war, but Chamberlain had done little to muster the Trade Unions. Bevin was not afraid to call on the Union leaders. On 26 May he summoned 2,000 representatives from 150 Unions. He told them that as socialists they must place themselves at the disposal of the state. They must go back to their factories and make sure that their fellow workers felt that they were partners in a great national enterprise. He asked for their support in the difficult job that lay ahead, and they gave it to him with enthusiasm. An Emergency Powers Bill granted the government complete control of persons and property while the war lasted and placed enormous power in the hands of the Minister of Labour. To begin with Bevin used his authority sparingly. He believed that once a man was in uniform he expected to obey orders, but that in civilian life he would expect to have freedom of choice. Therefore he saw two separate tasks in the future: the first to provide enough men to make the munitions, and the second to provide others to use them against the enemy – with both groups satisfied that they were playing an essential part in winning the war.

Bevin made a point of involving the Trade Union leaders in decisions at every level. They worked with the government, the managements and the men. Through this wartime experience they gained authority in industrial, economic and social matters that they have never lost, no matter what political party is in power.

Once the British people went into action under resolute leadership morale was high on the home front.

The German bombing of their towns and cities drew them together in dogged defiance. With the threat of imminent cross-Channel invasion the country became an island fortress, with every man, woman and child ready to fight Nazi tyranny. No one in Britain had wanted to go to war, but once they were in it they were determined not to be beaten. When British communists who might have caused trouble for the Trade Unions in the factories heard of Hitler's treacherous attack on the Soviet Union they worked with a will to turn out weapons to defeat him.

By 1941 skilled labour was in short supply everywhere. New factories were coming into operation; shipyards and mines were working overtime; food was becoming very scarce and the farmers were striving to raise more; the armed forces were increasing steadily and civil defence was an obvious necessity. Bevin realized that the time had come for sterner measures, and he thought that the national mood was ripe to receive them. He had to face up to the fact that unless he conscripted women he would never get the number of workers he needed. After grave consideration he took a bold decision – and it worked. He

From 1941 women entered the factories and the armed forces
in large numbers

directed unmarried women between eighteen and sixty and men who were not already employed to register for some form of national service. They responded readily and the public approved of compulsion, for it meant that everyone was treated alike and no one could escape their duty. Women went into factories, offices and canteens, trained for the auxiliary branches of the army, navy and air force, repaired machines and drove buses. They took on jobs that they had never done before and they did them well.

On 7 December 1941 Japanese bombers attacked without warning the United States fleet in the naval base of Pearl Harbor in the Pacific island of Hawaii, and left it in ruins. The news hit the world like a thunderclap, for no one had seen it coming. The following day the United States, Britain and the Commonwealth and China declared war on Japan. A vast conflict encircled the globe and Britain was no longer alone. Ever since he had taken office Winston Churchill had kept in close touch with Franklin Roosevelt, President of the United States. Roosevelt was wholeheartedly pro-British and anti-Nazi and he had given Britain all aid short of actually going to war. Now the two leaders were allies sharing their perils, their strength and their faith in final victory.

As the war dragged on the British Trade Unions increased in size and importance. They were concerned in every aspect of war production. Bevin worked with the labour leaders as a Minister and a friend. But however hard they tried they could not prevent unofficial strikes and stoppages. There was trouble in the Liverpool docks and Bevin spoke to the men straight. He told them: 'No other nation has ever been mobilized or disciplined to the extent of this nation. We have had a few strikes, not many. I do not want any more. I say to the Trade Unionists of this country: you may get your irritations in the factories, but don't stop work from now on either in mines, factory, dock or anywhere else for one minute. You don't hurt me, you don't

A party of 'Bevin Boys' begin their training at a colliery near Doncaster in 1943

hurt the government, but that single minute may mean the life of one of your sons in the fighting field.' They took it from him because he was one of them.

The strain of the war on the miners was more severe than on any other body of workers. The older men were very tired, their rations were not sufficient for the work they did, and they earned less money than the munition workers. They were divided between their patriotism and the long-standing wrongs that had never been righted. A wartime Ministry of Fuel and Power raised their wages and the protests subsided. The ministry also drafted boys of military age into the mines by ballot. They were known as the 'Bevin Boys'. They were not used to the work and most of them hated it, but it did keep coal production up to an essential level.

By the spring of 1945 victory was in sight and Hitler was retreating on every front. The Russians closed in on Berlin from one side, the British, Americans and the recently liberated French from the other. On 29 April Hitler shot himself and a week later the German Commander-in-Chief signed an unconditional surrender. The war in Europe was ended, but the war against Japan had still to be won. It took the Americans months of murderous fighting and the terrible decision to drop two atomic bombs before the Japanese surrendered.

Meanwhile in Britain there had been a general election. Despite Winston Churchill's war record the Labour party won a sweeping victory.

Thus Churchill and Bevin ended their partnership. They had worked closely together for five years and proved an invincible team. Each one had been totally loyal to the other through times of intense crisis and acute anxiety. They viewed each other with respect, but they were never intimate. The difference in their backgrounds was too great. It was not possible to bridge the gap between the wealthy aristocrat and the poor boy who made good.

Before Churchill resigned he wrote Bevin a letter of great sincerity offering him the Order of Merit, one of the greatest honours he could confer. Bevin wrote back with gratitude and grace refusing the offer. He had completed the job he set out to do. He had organized labour with remarkable skill and added greatly to the status of the Trade Unions. He was happy to remain plain Mr Bevin.

16 The Welfare State

The Labour party fought the 1945 election on a Manifesto called 'Let us Face the Future'. It set out in great detail a programme for full employment, high production, better housing and greatly improved social services. It also undertook to nationalize the Bank of England, the mines, the fuel and power industries, inland transport and iron and steel. The Manifesto was widely read and carried great weight, and the Labour policy was strongly supported by the Unions. Many people held the Conservative government responsible for the mass unemployment between the two wars and were determined that it should not happen again. They respected Churchill as a superb war leader, but now they were turning their minds to peace.

Labour won 393 seats which gave them a majority of 146 over all other parties. The Liberal party had faded to a shadow with only twelve seats.

The Labour party had changed its character. It no longer recruited its members solely from the working class. A third of the candidates were put up by the Trades Unions and the other two thirds were youngish middle-class professional men, and some women: lawyers, journalists, scientists, doctors and teachers. Many had been educated at public schools and universities and rose rapidly to Cabinet rank.

Clement Attlee became Prime Minister and Ernest Bevin Foreign Secretary. Attlee had grown up as a Conservative, but he was converted to socialism by the sight of the appalling poverty of the London slums, and by contact with the social reformers Sidney and Beatrice Webb. He became a settlement worker in the East End, and fought through the First World War before he turned to politics as a career.

The nationalization process went smoothly through Parliament. First, the government took over control of the Bank of England, then it formed the National Coal Board, fulfilling the long-standing demands of the miners. In 1947 the British Transport Commission reorganized the railways and canals, which were already working at a loss, and road haulage transport. In 1948 electricity and gas came under public ownership. All these changes were approved by the Trade Unions concerned. The nationalization of the iron and steel industry was more controversial. It was tied up with so many other sections of industry, and as it was making a reasonable profit the owners were reluctant to give it up. Finally the government agreed to buy up the iron and steel companies, but not to put nationalization into effect until after the next election. In this way Labour completed its programme of public ownership. Though the Unions

Clement Attlee   Arthur Deakin

opposed private enterprise they soon realized that running these nationalized industries was a full-time job for competent men. They lost many able officials who left to staff government boards and commissions. This, however, had its compensations because these former Trades Union officials as heads of government-run industries faced the same problems as heads of non-nationalized industries and were thinking along the same lines. For instance, though Bevin resigned as Secretary of the Transport Workers' Union and Chairman of the General Council to become Minister of Labour during the Second World War, he never lost touch with Union problems. Bevin was succeeded in both positions by Arthur Deakin, a moderate Trade Unionist who shared many of his ideas.

Meanwhile Labour leaders were paying a great deal of attention to the social services. In 1942, at the request of the coalition government, William Beveridge, a distinguished economist and specialist in social problems, had published a blueprint for a Welfare State. In 1946 the National Insurance and the National Health Service Acts came into force. Both were based on the recommendations of the Beveridge Report. The National Insurance Act provided unemployment and sickness benefits for everyone in the country, through the weekly contributions of the employers, the employees and the state. Women received a pension at sixty and men at sixty-five, and parents got a family allowance for every child except the first.

The National Health Service was steered through the House of Commons by Aneurin Bevan, an ex-miner who was a most forceful Minister of Health. It provided free treatment and drugs for all. The hospitals were nationalized and National Health doctors received an annual payment for each patient who registered on their panels. Through their weekly contributions everybody in Britain was entitled to the best medical care that existed in the country. It reduced the fear of illness, and lifted a great financial burden from the minds of many families.

119

William Beveridge   Ellen Wilkinson

Ellen Wilkinson, who had led the Jarrow March, was the Minister of Education. She succeeded in raising the school leaving age to fifteen, and in providing university grants for students who could not possibly afford to go otherwise.

Certain Conservative critics of these Acts claimed that the British were becoming too soft – 'protected from the cradle to the grave'. But most middle- and working-class people in Britain were thankful for government aid, and a financial security they had never had before.

A Welfare State is costly to run, and Sir Stafford Cripps, who had recently been appointed Chancellor of the Exchequer, was forced to introduce rigid economies in spending in order to balance the national budget. He clamped down on shopping sprees by taxing home products and thus raising the prices of goods in the shops. He restricted imports so that few tempting foreign goods came into the country. He fixed overseas currency allowances for individuals at such a low level that the British could not spend expensive holidays abroad. And, most important of all, with some difficulty, he persuaded a number of

120

Unions to accept 'a wage restraint' – an agreement not to strike for higher wages.

The General Council of the TUC was anxious to support government policy. But a few fanatical communists were creating serious disunity in industry. They had been able to work their way into key positions in the Unions during the war because they were seen to be determined to defeat Hitler at any price. Once the fighting ended with the Soviet Union victorious, they resumed their battle against the British way of life and what they termed 'the curse of capitalism'.

In the 1945 election only two communists were elected to Parliament. But they had political influence which far exceeded their numbers. By 1947 communist officials controlled the Electrical Trades Union, the Foundry Workers and the Fire Brigades Union. Nine openly declared members of the Communist party sat on the board of the Transport and General Workers' Union, until Arthur Deakin revealed their revolutionary tactics and got them all dismissed at the end of 1949. The political confrontations with the communists were sharpened by the 'Cold War' which cut off the Soviet Union and the satellite communist states from the democratic nations of the West.

In June 1947 General George Marshall, the American Secretary of State, outlined a remarkable plan to help the war-damaged countries rebuild their economies. Each nation, according to its means, would contribute to its own recovery and the United States would back them up. During the following five years the United States Congress voted the vast sum of $20,000,000,000 to help European reconstruction. The Marshall Plan was offered to allies and enemies alike. The Americans did not impose conditions or try to dictate a way of life but they hoped that if people were prosperous and at peace they would not fall for communist propaganda or submit to communist domination.

Stalin refused Marshall Aid for the Soviet Union and also

for East Germany, Czechoslovakia, Poland and the other satellite states under communist control. He was afraid that if they got help from America they might suspect that the 'cruel capitalists' were not as evil as he had painted them. In Winston Churchill's words, Stalin lowered an 'Iron Curtain' cutting off all normal communication between the Soviet Union and the West.

The World Federation of Trade Unions which had included the Soviet Union, Britain and many other European countries, split on the conflicting attitudes to the Marshall Plan. In the West it was replaced by the International Confederation of Free Trade Unions which excluded the communists but included the American Congress of Industrial Organization and the American Federation of Labor which had long been on very good terms with Britain.

After five years in office the British Labour leaders had achieved almost everything they had planned. Their success was largely due to Clement Attlee, a modest man who managed to get things done. The Trade Unions had strengthened their position in the country and there had been few strikes. Many industries had introduced the 'closed shop', refusing to employ workers who were not Union members. Non-Unionists criticized this practice, but the Union leaders argued that it was unfair that workers who did not join should enjoy the privileges that Union members had sacrificed so much to win.

Early in 1950 there was a general election and Attlee was confident that the country was behind him. However, people were tired of austerity and Labour scraped in with a bare majority of nine seats. It was evident that another election would soon follow and 1950 was a bad year for Labour leaders. Both Ernest Bevin and Stafford Cripps resigned owing to ill health and died soon afterwards. Aneurin Bevan and Harold Wilson resigned because the Chancellor of the Exchequer put a charge on false teeth, and Clement Attlee had to go into hospital. The party was left in poor shape and the following year the Conservatives won an election with a majority of seventeen seats.

Labour was out of office for thirteen years, and during this time the Trade Unions were more active in competing with each other than in fighting for their industrial rights. The Welfare State had taken the wind out of the 'protest for progress' campaign. Strikes were frequent and unpopular with the public. In the mid-fifties a printing strike stopped all newspapers, followed by a train strike. A Gallup Poll showed that both Conservative and Labour voters felt that the government was being too lenient with the Unions. There was a storm in the Electrical Trades Union where moderate leaders claimed and then established in court that the communists were faking ballot papers to get their men in. Finally the ETU was expelled from the TUC.

In March 1958 the General Council of the TUC held a ceremonial opening of Congress House, the new London headquarters. The handsome modern building was a memorial to the Trade Unionists who had died in the war and a tribute to the many able and devoted leaders who had guided the Unions in times of trouble. Despite their rivalries and unrest they stood for equality and justice. In 1962 a Gallup Poll reported that two out of every three people who had been questioned agreed that on the whole the Trade Unions 'were a good thing'.

17   How the Trade Unions Work

By October 1964 the Conservatives had been in office for thirteen years, having increased their majority at two successive elections. They were then compelled to hold another election because their legal five-year term of government was running out. The opinion polls showed that throughout the country, the Conservative and Labour parties were closely matched. It proved to be an accurate forecast, for when the votes were counted Labour had a majority of only five seats.

Harold Wilson had led his party to victory with skill and determination. He was, at that time, the outstanding Labour leader and he became Prime Minister at the age of forty-eight. He had already made a name for himself as a formidable debater for the Opposition in the House of Commons. Despite his narrow majority he set out boldly to bring about the changes he felt were needed. Labour inherited a poor economic situation and was forced to set up a national board to control prices and incomes, and report on its findings. It was an unpopular but necessary measure.

In 1965 the Labour government persuaded the General Council of the TUC to agree to the appointment of a Royal Commission to study the whole question of industrial relations and the Trade Unions in particular.

Eleven commissioners, under their Chairman Lord Donovan, an Appeal Court judge and former Labour MP, were appointed 'to consider the relations between managements and employees and the role of Trade Unions and employers' associations in

Harold Wilson

promoting the interests of their members and accelerating the social and economic growth of the nation, with particular reference to the law affecting the bodies; and to report'. In simple words the government wanted to cut down the number of strikes and turn out more goods.

The Donovan Commission took three years to complete its thorough and detailed document. Though certain Acts have changed the relationship between the government, the employers and the Trade Unions it still stands as a record of the way that Trade Unions work.

The last Royal Commission on working relations had reported sixty-two years earlier, and during that period two world wars had brought about big changes in the structure of British industry. Coal, cotton and railways had shrunk in importance; and oil, synthetic fibres and motor cars had been produced in large quantities and taken their place in the Trade Union world.

125

The number of Trade Union members had quadrupled from $2\frac{1}{2}$ million in 1908 to 10 million in 1964; they then formed nearly half of all employees in the country. The Donovan Commission reported on the size of the Unions and they varied greatly from the Transport and General Workers' Union, with 1,482,000 members, to the Jewish Bakers' Union with twenty-four. As machinery grows more efficient and organization more compli- cated, the proportion of technicians and white-collar workers increases and the proportion of manual workers diminishes. Teachers, accountants, computer operators, civil servants and many other office workers have formed Unions which did not exist fifty years ago. They all paid a weekly contribution to Trade Union funds which provided strike pay when necessary and sometimes also provided convalescent homes, training centres and other benefits for its members. In some cases they built up a political fund to pay the election expenses of a Trade Union candidate. Almost invariably there was also a political levy to provide funds for the Labour party. The contributions varied from Union to Union as they do today, and they are fixed by the particular Trade Union according to the means of its members and the benefits they expect to receive.

The commissioners recognized two systems of industrial negotiation: the first formal and the second informal. The first is a system whereby an industry, such as the printers or boiler- makers, forms an association of employers to decide on a scale of pay, hours of work, overtime earnings and length of holidays. The Association then presents these terms to the Union leaders of the same industry for negotiation at a national level. The resulting terms then apply to all employers and all workers in the industry. The second is a system by which many of these decisions are taken within individual factories and according to local conditions. Many managers follow an established pat- tern of 'custom and practice' based on long-term experience of what is acceptable to employers and employees alike.

The formal system appeared outdated in 1964 and it works badly today. It is often detached from current conditions and indifferent to particular needs. The informal system is more human in its approach and more adaptable.

Within the factories the negotiations proceed at various levels. Many personnel managers whom employers appoint are specially trained to deal with industrial problems. They spend their time supervising pay structures and act as general consultants in times of trouble. The full-time Trade Union officials are elected by the workers to represent their interests. They are the official links between the men and the management. They attend the yearly Trades Union Congress, and help to form Trade Union policy. They are paid a regular salary for their services according to their ability and the funds available.

The shop stewards work on a different level and they are very important indeed. They are picked by their workmates to deal with every kind of factory problem. It is not a full-time job in itself. Some factories compensate them for the hours they have to take off work to devote to Union affairs, while others expect them to give their services free. Because they are on the spot they can sometimes catch a crisis early before it creates real trouble. They take part in everyday matters, like the length of tea breaks and collecting Union contributions, and they are on hand if workers have to change their jobs, if a works manager takes on fresh labour or the owners install new machinery. Little by little they have taken on more responsibility and exerted more power. A militant shop steward can cause considerable trouble in a factory and a wise one can smooth out most difficulties.

The managers could well have resented the influence of the shop stewards, but the Donovan survey showed that in general they welcomed their help. If the shop stewards can persuade the workers to accept a fair compromise at work-bench level the management is grateful. If the shop stewards fail they contact their Union leaders. In this case the Union officials together with the managers have the authority to make final decisions. Both state-owned concerns and private companies have boards of directors supervising the working of British industry. But however experienced and high-powered they are they cannot do it alone. Production depends on efficient machines, but even more on the goodwill and cooperation of the men and women who operate them. Without Trade Union agreement and support it is very likely to drop.

Unofficial strikes are frequent and wasteful. They occur when the shop stewards either lose control or take sides with the strikers before the appropriate Union official has a chance of settling the dispute. Once the dispute reaches an official level, 'collective bargaining' is probably the best means of settling it. This means that a chosen representative of a state-owned industry or an employers' association meets a chosen representative of the Trade Union to sort out the knotty problem. They are both experienced in the field and well briefed for the occasion. They have to be both loyal to their own colleagues and aware of national needs. In present day 'collective bargaining' the negotiators seldom aim at complete victory for themselves or defeat for the other side. Instead they seek and usually find a middle way.

The Donovan commissioners also reported on the long-established system of apprenticeship. For hundreds of years craftsmen had learned and perfected their skills over a period of years, and emerged independent, masters of their trade. But with a good education, modern machinery and improved techniques a willing worker can probably learn a skill in a few months. If he is limited by a long apprenticeship he will probably be underemployed for years; and he may well find that by the time he is allowed to work as a fully trained man methods have changed and the original job no longer exists.

Therefore training and retraining have become an accepted

part of working life. As one industry declines and another grows, workers may have to learn new jobs, move house and put their children into new schools. But with a system of state aid and Trade Union support to tide over the change they do not have to go on the dole.

Perhaps the most important of all the Donovan recommendations related to the place of legal action in industrial disputes. The commissioners advised against increasing the powers of the law to make agreements legally binding and to enforce factory discipline. They considered that informal consultation and collective bargaining were the best ways of promoting well-being at work, raising production and balancing the national budget. Though they admitted the process was far from perfect they did not think it would be improved by accusing men and women who stopped work because they had a grievance of breaking the law, fining them or sending them to prison. Industry is made up of a vast, complex mixture of people, and no law can compel them to get along happily together.

In the debate on the report in the House of Commons the Labour party was seriously divided. Public opinion was critical of the Trade Unions and angered by the recent strikes. But a large section of the Labour movement opposed the idea put forward by a number of MPs of granting legal powers to the state to enforce industrial discipline. Harold Wilson, the Prime Minister, and Barbara Castle, his Secretary for Employment and Productivity, favoured the use of the law and fought hard for their convictions. Finally they had to give in because it was clear that if they persisted they would split the Labour party, which would then be defeated in the House of Commons and lose the power to take any action at all. The proposed legislation was therefore withdrawn and the Trade Unions remained in very much the same position they had held before.

18   The Present and the Future

In a general election on 18 June 1970 the Conservative party under Edward Heath turned out the Labour government that had been in office since 1964. The Conservatives returned to power with a majority of thirty-one seats over all other parties.

In Britain in 1970 there were more strikes than in any year since 1926, the year of the 'General Strike'. The most important disputes were the three-week dock strike in July and August, the six-week stoppage of local authority manual workers, and a ban by workers on overtime in the electricity supply industry during December.

The beginning of the 1970s found the Trade Union movement in an uncompromising mood. A relatively new group of Trade Union leaders faced Robert Carr, the new Conservative Secretary of Employment and Productivity, who had made an election promise to introduce new legislation on industrial relations if the Conservatives came to power. The government's Industrial Relations Act came into force in 1971. It was the most far-reaching law dealing with industrial relations that had ever been passed through the British Parliament. It was debated for fifty-six days and was the centre of bitter political dispute.

The new Act set up machinery for Industrial Courts and established a framework of rules for management, Trade Unions, and individuals. It gave the workers new rights that protected them against unfair dismissal from their jobs. It also provided for a 'cooling off' period of sixty days when a strike threatened to create a crisis for the nation.

Thousands of trade unionists march in support of the five jailed dockers, 25 July 1972

The most serious disputes which arose under the Act would be handled by an Industrial Court which had the status of a High Court. Trade Unions had to register in order to benefit from the Act. But many Trade Unionists were afraid that the law would interfere with their freedom to bargain with employers. The TUC at its annual congress voted to instruct Unions not to register.

The passing of this law was followed by a serious worsening of labour relations. In July 1972 five British dockers were imprisoned for defying the orders of the Industrial Relations Court by picketing the premises of a container firm. By that same evening 26,000 dockers came out on strike as a protest. Other unions came out in sympathy and three days later no national newspapers were printed in London. The General Council of the TUC voted to call a one-day general strike a week later. The same evening the Industrial Court ordered the release of the dockers and the strike was called off. Five months later in December 1972 engineering workers protested in a series of strikes against a fine of £50,000 imposed on their Union by the Industrial Relations Court.

The other major cause of the workers' discontent was the government pay policy which was imposed on the nationalized industries. The government aimed to limit wage increases in these industries in the hope that private industry would follow suit. This pay policy was extremely unpopular among the workers in the nationalized industries. In January 1972 a strike of coal miners, the first national coal strike since 1926, lasted fifty days. The miners picketed electricity generating stations and this led to extensive power cuts in industry and between $1\frac{1}{2}$ million and 2 million people were put out of work. The miners claimed pay increases of up to 47 per cent. The National Coal Board offered between 7 and 8 per cent which the miners promptly rejected. The dispute was submitted to a court of inquiry which came to the conclusion that the miners' claim for 'a general and exceptional increase' was reasonable. The court finally recommended an increase of 25 per cent which the miners accepted. In the same year the Post Office workers struck for forty-seven days.

In November 1973 the electrical workers and the miners revolted against the pay policy and banned overtime. Meanwhile the long-standing enmity between the Israelis and Arabs in the Middle East broke out into open warfare. The Arabs imposed an embargo on oil supplies to Western Europe and the United States to discourage these countries from giving any support to Israel. A month later a serious shortage of electrical power led to the government decision to reduce electricity supplies to industry to three days a week.

In February 1974 the National Union of Mineworkers decided to call an all-out strike for higher wages. Under the Industrial Relations Act the government demanded a ballot among

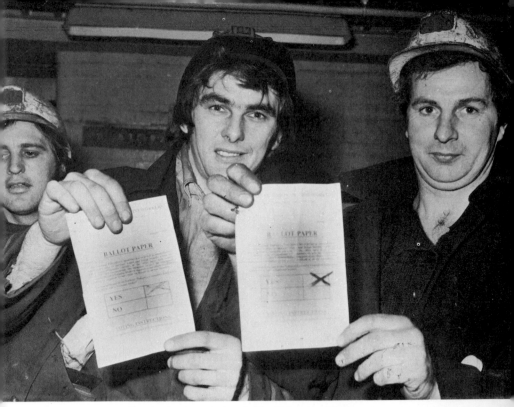

Kent miners vote to strike, February 1974

the miners and this resulted in an 81 per cent support for the strike. Two days later Edward Heath called for a general election. Though he had a small, but workable, majority in Parliament he felt he needed greater support from the country in his fight against inflation and the pressures of militant Trade Unionists.

Harold Wilson continued to lead the Labour party. He fought the election on a programme that included the renegotiation of British membership of the Common Market, a wide-ranging programme of reform to help low income groups, increased public ownership of industry, and the repeal of the Conservatives' Industrial Relations Act which had led to so much conflict.

The election ended in a deadlock. Labour was the largest single party with a majority of only five members over the Conservatives. This majority could, at any moment, be reversed by the thirty-seven members of other small parties. Edward Heath resigned and the Queen called on Harold Wilson to form a

Labour government. Though this government was very insecure it succeeded in fulfilling its major pledge to the Trade Unions by repealing the Industrial Relations Act. Harold Wilson settled the coal strike immediately by granting the enormous wage increases that the miners demanded. A few weeks later the state of emergency ended and a five-day working week was resumed.

It was clear that Labour would have difficulty in running the country with such a small working majority. Therefore Harold Wilson decided to hold another election in October. The main feature of his election manifesto was a 'Social Contract' between a Labour government and the Trade Unions. The main object of the 'Social Contract' was to encourage the Trade Unions voluntarily to accept smaller wage increases. The Trades Union Congress as a body was in favour of this agreement. However, some Unions such as the Amalgamated Union of Engineering Workers and the National Union of Mineworkers were uncertain.

The election which took place in October 1974 increased the Labour majority to forty-three seats over the Conservatives, but with a majority of only three seats over all parties. Harold Wilson continued as Prime Minister. The government at once found itself in grave difficulties because of the financial state of the country. The money that was being spent by the nation on public services such as the Post Office, by local authorities on housing and schools, and in nationalized industries such as coal and railways, had to be carefully controlled. The result was a large increase in postal and telephone charges, gas and electricity prices, and in fares on railways and buses. The government sought the cooperation of the Trades Union Congress, for without it there would certainly have been further strikes. Eventually it was agreed that for one year no one should have a pay increase of more than £6 a week. While these discussions were taking place unemployment rose from 742,000 in January to 1,230,000 in August 1975.

James Callaghan

Harold Wilson resigned as Prime Minister in March 1976. Although he had told the Queen of his decision three months earlier, his resignation came as a complete surprise to the nation.

Three weeks later James Callaghan, after being elected party leader by the Labour Members of Parliament, was invited by Queen Elizabeth to become Prime Minister. He had started his working life as a clerk in the Inland Revenue, and during the Second World War he had joined the navy and had risen to be a lieutenant in Naval Intelligence. When the war ended James Callaghan turned to politics and was elected to Parliament as Labour Member for Cardiff. In the Wilson governments of 1964–1970 he held posts as Chancellor of the Exchequer and Home Secretary. In 1974 he had moved to the Foreign Office where he had taken charge of the renegotiations with the Common Market.

Soon after James Callaghan became Prime Minister a new Budget was introduced in which the Chancellor of the Exchequer proposed that when the £6 limit on pay increases came to an end there should be a 3 per cent wage increase limit in return for a reduction in taxes. This had to be debated with the Trade Unions in order to get their cooperation. A month later, after constant negotiation, the Unions agreed to a 4·5 per cent wage rise in return for cuts in income tax.

At the end of May 1976 the National Executive Committee published 'Labour's Programme for Britain' which outlined

135

what the Labour party considered a better deal for the working people. The Committee laid great stress on industrial democracy. The important section on economic planning contained the following recommendations:

1. That at all levels workers must take an active part in decision-making.

2. Joint regulations must go well beyond the wages and conditions of employment. 'Employers must be required to negotiate and agree with the Trade Union representatives ... over the entire operation of their firms and industries ... joint control is thus our first target: to cover all decisions at whatever level they are taken, from the shop floor up to and including the boardroom.'

3. 'But even where firms are highly unionized and where joint control is firmly established, we believe that further progress can be made. We believe that it should be in the direction of employees' control and self-management.'

Collective bargaining is not enough. 'We must establish formally the right of workers ... for joint control to be extended to areas like investment, mergers, pricing, employment and manpower policies.' Companies employing in the first instance over 2,000 workers must establish a Main Policy Board; of the seats available on this Board 50 per cent would be available for workers' representatives elected through their recognized Trade Union machinery.

This programme will not become official policy until it is included in the Election Manifesto issued before the next general election. But meanwhile the Labour government has reacted favourably to all its proposals for greater worker participation.

At the TUC Annual Congress in 1976 one of the main points for discussion was whether after a period of wage restraint, which was to last a further ten months, the Unions should return to the process of free collective bargaining.

136

Collective bargaining means that representatives of employers and the Unions try to come to terms over conditions of work and the level of wages. Therefore employers have to recognize the existence of the Unions and their right to strike. The workers have the power to withhold their labour against the economic power of the employers. Collective bargaining has been criticized by economists in recent years because it has led to constantly rising wages and therefore to constantly rising prices. As an alternative the government has tried to replace the system of collective bargaining by an overall agreement with the Trades Union Congress, such as the 'Social Contract'.

In October 1974 the TUC agreed to limit its demands for wage increases over the period of a year. After discussion this arrangement was continued for a second year. This agreement was based on the expectation of falling unemployment which in fact did not occur. As a result there were insistent demands at the Trades Union Congress in 1976 for a return to collective bargaining in the following year.

The Trade Unions have never been agreeable to long periods of wage restraint fixed by the government. On the other hand collective bargaining has in recent years been followed by rising prices. It appears that after the financial crises of the past few years some other form of agreement between the government, the Unions and the employers to settle wages will have to be found.

Presumably over the next few years a new system of negotiation will be developed representing all three bodies involved in industry: the Unions, the employers and the government. This system will have to work out a wages policy which recognizes the value of particular skills and the importance of being able to take responsibility. Any wages policy will also have to take into account its effect on the finances of the nation.

A just wages policy is a national, all-party problem that can be solved only with political goodwill and skilful negotiation.

137

Book List

Britain in the Century of Total War, Arthur Marwick, Bodley Head, 1968.
The Economics of Trade Unions, Albert Rees, University of Chicago Press, 1962.
A History of British Trade Unionism, Henry Pelling, Penguin Books, 1971.
A History of British Trade Unions since 1889, vol. I 1889–1910, H. A. Clegg, Alan Fox and A. F. Thompson, Clarendon Press, 1964.
The History of the T.U.C., 1868–1968, The General Council of the Trades Union Congress, 1968.
The History of Trade Unionism, Sidney and Beatrice Webb, Longmans Green, 1920.
The Industrial and Commercial Revolutions in Great Britain During the Nineteenth Century, L. C. A. Knowles, Routledge, 1926.
The Industrial Revolution 1750–1850, H. L. Beales, Cass, 1958.
The Labour Party: A Short History, Edward P. Wilmot, Macmillan, St Martin's Press, 1968.
The Life of Francis Place, Graham Wallas, Allen & Unwin, 1925.
The Life and Times of Ernest Bevin, vol. I, Alan Bullock, Heinemann, 1960.
The Making of the English Working Class, E. P. Thompson, Penguin Books, 1968.
Mayhew's London, edited by Peter Quennell, Pilot Press, 1949.
The Miners of South Wales, E. W. Evans, University of Wales Press, 1961.
Royal Commission on Trade Unions and Employers' Associations 1965–1968, Her Majesty's Stationery Office, reprinted 1975.
A Short History of the Labour Party, Henry Pelling, Macmillan, 1972.
The Tolpuddle Martyrs, Marjorie Firth and Arthur W. Hopkinson, Martin Hopkinson Ltd, 1934.
The Town Labourer 1760–1832, J. L. Hammond and Barbara Hammond, Longmans Green, 1920.
Trade Unions, Eric Wigham, Oxford University Press, 1969.
The Trade Unions, the Employers and the State, Harry Welton, Pall Mall Press, 1960.
Trade Unions, Growth, Structure and Policy, H. A. Turner, Allen & Unwin, 1962.
Victorian People, Asa Briggs, Penguin Books, 1965.
Village Life and Labour, edited by Raphael Samuel, Routledge & Kegan Paul, 1975.
What's Wrong with the Unions?, Eric Wigham, Penguin Books, 1961.
1868: Year of the Unions, Edmund Frow and Michael Katanka, Michael Katanka Books Ltd, 1968.

Index

Index

Index